THE OFFICIAL **NATIONAL PARK GUIDE**

BRECON BEACONS

TEXT BY **ROGER THOMAS** · PHOTOGRAPHS BY **HARRY WILLIAMS**

SERIES EDITOR ROLY SMITH

PEVENSEY GUIDES

The Pevensey Press is an imprint of
David & Charles

First published in the UK in 2002

Map artwork by Ethan Danielson
based on material supplied by the
Brecon Beacons National Park
Authority

A catalogue record for this book is
available from the British Library.

ISBN 1 898630 19 4 (paperback)

Edited by Sue Viccars
Book design by Les Dominey Design
Company, Exeter
and Printed in China by
CT Printing Ltd.
for David & Charles
Brunel House Newton Abbot Devon

Contents

Page 1: Walkers on the hillside above Llangattock, with Pen Cerrig-calch in the distance
Pages 2–3: The peaceful Dyffryn Crawnon valley, hidden away below Mynydd Llangynidr
Left: Isolated farmstead in the central Beacons

Front cover (above): The central Beacons rise to 2,907ft (886m) at Pen y fan, the highest summit in south Wales; (below) Cwmyoy's tipsy church, a victim of subsidence, is anything but upright; (front flap) Llandovery's attractive old marketplace
Back cover: Overlooking the foothills of the unexplored Black Mountain

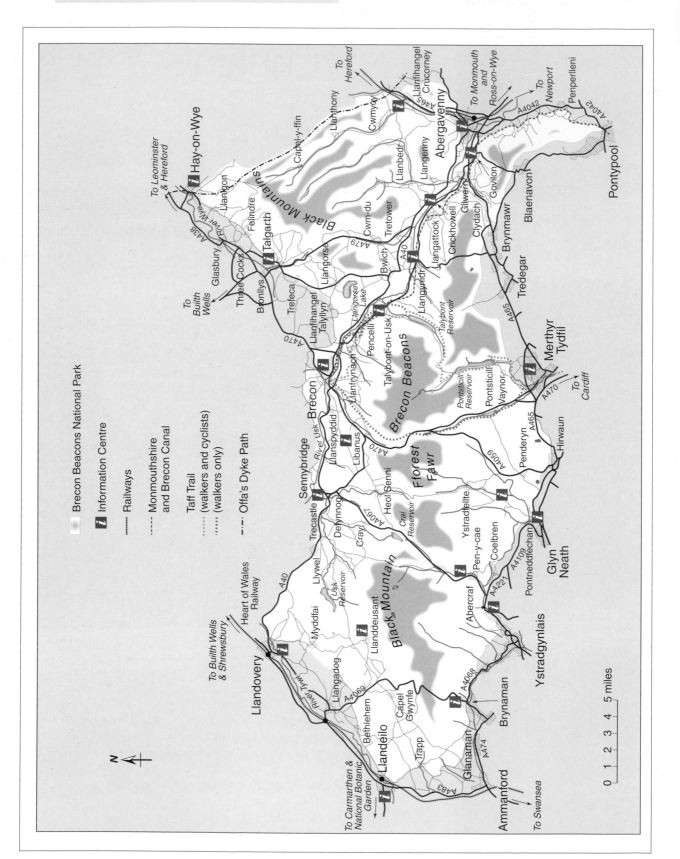

Key

- Brecon Beacons National Park
- *i* Information Centre
- Railways
- Monmouthshire and Brecon Canal
- Taff Trail (walkers and cyclists)
- (walkers only)
- Offa's Dyke Path

N

0 1 2 3 4 5 miles

Foreword

By Martin Fitton, Chief Executive, Association of National Park Authorities

The Brecon Beacons National Park is one of our finest landscapes, ranging from the wide Usk valley in the east, to the small traditional farms in the west. The whole is linked by the backbone of the Black Mountains in the east; the central Beacons; and (perhaps confusingly) the Black Mountain in the west, all of which dominate the valleys of urban south Wales. Diverse in landscape, it is also diverse in its culture. In the west, a largely Welsh-speaking population mostly earns a living from traditional farming. In the east, the Park looks towards England and shares many characteristics of the border country.

Our National Parks are doubly special. Unlike many in the world, they are landscapes created, and largely maintained, by humans, mainly through farming. They are 'living landscapes' where change occurs through development in the small towns and villages and through changes in agricultural and forestry practices.

Change has not always worked to the advantage of the National Parks. For example, if you had visited the Beacons fifty years ago, you would have seen a great deal more heather on the hillside than you do now – the result of increased grazing encouraged by agricultural policies introduced after World War II, obliging farmers to produce more in order to maintain an adequate standard of living. The policies are now changing, however, and the role farmers play in maintaining these beautiful landscapes is now recognised and funding is being provided to help them – although not yet enough.

Similarly, while the towns and villages in the Park have changed over the years, the way in which new development has been fitted amicably into existing communities is quite visible, and overall the quality and beauty of the area has been maintained, helped by the protection offered by its National Park status. So when you visit the Park, remember that you are not simply looking at a beautiful landscape. You are seeing a place where people have lived and worked over many centuries.

National Parks are now cared for by independent planning authorities which hold land, provide grants to farmers and others; provide rangers, information, car parks and toilets; clear footpaths and litter, plant trees and partner many other agencies in pursuit of the purposes for which they exist. They are there to conserve natural beauty, wildlife and cultural heritage and to promote the Parks' enjoyment by the public while fostering the social and economic well-being of their residents.

As a visitor, you can help sustain this wonderful landscape. Simply by being there, you are helping the local economy. You can help even more if you make a special effort to find and purchase local goods and services. Celebrate the fact that this is an environment producing good quality local food. This will mean that you become a more 'sustainable' tourist – a jargon word that expresses the challenging thought that we can look after the environment while enjoying the beauty of the countryside.

You have probably arrived by car or intend to travel by car in the National Park. Once you get to the Park, consider leaving your car behind during at least part of your visit. You will enjoy the Park much more if you get out and walk through its landscapes, and stop and chat to those you meet, instead of trying to see everything in one visit.

In all of these ways, you can help protect the National Park while enjoying its beauty and tranquillity. It is a pleasure to welcome you.

Introducing the Brecon Beacons

I have a long and enduring relationship with the Brecon Beacons. My childhood was spent within sight of the soaring, flat-topped summits of the central Beacons and I now live in the Usk valley on the eastern flank of the National Park. When I was young I attached no special significance to the fact that within ten minutes of my terraced village in the industrial mining valleys I could be crossing the Park boundary into a different world. To a youngster brought up in the area it was no Great Divide, despite the dramatic – and sudden – contrast between the sprawling industrialisation of the valleys and the wild, open slopes of the Beacons. For me, the crossing of that barrier – marked by the sign of the flaming beacon – raised few thoughts other than the prospect of another hill to climb, or waterfall to visit.

Above: A shepherd from the central Brecons

Left: Gospel Pass, Black Mountains

Nowadays, of course, it's all a little different. I was ten years of age when the Brecon Beacons National Park came into existence in April 1957. I'm now well versed in the dialogue between conservation and recreation, preservation and exploitation. Arguments supporting sustainability and the need to protect our beautiful spaces are rarely out of the headlines. We live in environmentally aware times.

If you'd told me all those years ago that the high and mighty Beacons, the tallest, toughest, roughest peaks in south Wales, were an extremely fragile environment, I wouldn't have known what you were talking about. The boundless Beacons, with their swooping escarpments, glacial tarns, wild moorlands and huge vistas? Fragile? Pull the other one.

This preamble is by way of making the point that the boundary which truly defines the Brecon Beacons National Park is its southern one. The sudden transition from industrial to rural Wales – where the old, coal-bearing valleys run up against the moors, hill-sheep farms and forests of the Beacons – constitutes the *raison d'être* of this particular National Park.

THE GREAT DIVIDE

Nowhere is the divide more emphatic than along the A465 'Heads of the Valleys' road between Abergavenny and Merthyr Tydfil, a route which, in effect, serves as part of the southern boundary. North of the road swathes of empty moorland roll away uninterrupted into the foothills of the Beacons. To the south, an untidy scattering of terraced towns and villages occupy a some-

Maen Madoc standing stone on Sarn Helen Roman road, Fforest Fawr

what scrappy, pock-marked landscape that still bears evidence of intense industrialisation despite the clean-up schemes of the last few decades.

Most of Wales's 2¾ million inhabitants live in the relatively confined spaces of the south east, between the Brecon Beacons and the sea. Despite the death of coalmining (it's not quite dead and buried – one pit remains) and decline of heavy industry, it's also true to say that most of Wales's economic activity is still concentrated here, in and around Cardiff, along the M4 corridor and up into the industrial valleys. And it is all, of course, worryingly close to the Brecon Beacons. Nowadays, with road improvements, you can drive from Cardiff, bypassing Merthyr Tydfil, and be at the boundary of the National Park in about half an hour. When the Park was designated in 1957 that journey would have taken a little longer, but the message was – and still is – loud and clear: the future for the Beacons as an inviolate area lies in its protected status as a National Park.

The Beacons' other boundaries are, in pure landscape terms, a little less self-determined. To the east, they are contiguous with the Wales/England border, while to the north the Rivers Wye, Usk and the army's Mynydd Epynt military training ranges help draw the lines on the map. In the west, the River Tywi and the country town of Llandeilo mark the edge of the Park. All in all, the Park stretches for over 40 miles (64km) from the Welsh border to the fringes of Swansea, encompassing an area of 519sq miles (1,344sq km).

The Brecon Beacons is a Park of consistent character. Imagine, if you can, wave after wave of open mountainside, rising and dipping fluidly across the landscape like some giant, petrified green sea. Although a mountainous area, these highlands have little in common with their northern counterpart in the

Snowdonia National Park, where a lucky-dip landscape of boulder-strewn slopes, jagged pinnacles, boggy moors and wooded valleys changes by the mile. In comparison, the Beacons are reassuringly uncomplicated and homogenous. In topographical terms, this is a Park of few surprises, of highland pure and simple. There is a fundamental simplicity and solidity about the Beacons, qualities underlined by the wide, open spaces and big skies that are such a feature of this part of Wales.

If there are any grounds for complexity it lies in the etymology of the Park. The place names here seem designed to confuse. For a start, let's take the name of the Park itself. The Brecon Beacons refer not only to the entire Park but also to just one of four distinct upland ranges within its boundaries. Then there's the perennial case of mistaken identity – occasionally aided and abetted by even the most pedantic of guidebooks – surrounding the Black Mountains (plural) and the Black Mountain (singular). Confused? You should be.

For the record, the quartet of mountain ranges within the National Park are as follows, running from east to west: first comes the Black Mountains, the lofty chain of hills along the Wales/England border; next in line are the Brecon Beacons, occupying the heart of the Park; moving westwards we then reach the moors and plateaux of Fforest Fawr; then, in the far west, there's the Black Mountain, a daunting wilderness area made up of the loneliest landscapes in south Wales.

Throughout this book, I'll aim for consistency when I refer to the Beacons. The Brecon Beacons or simply 'Beacons' can be taken to mean the entire

Cascading waterfall on the River Mellte, near Ystradfellte

Far-reaching views across the Usk valley and Black Mountains from the hills above Crickhowell

National Park; when I write about the actual mountain range I'll use the term 'central Beacons'.

A CONSISTENT CHARACTER

The uniformity displayed by the Brecon Beacons derives from the nature of the underlying rock, Old Red Sandstone, which divides the ancient rocks of central Wales from the south Wales coalfield. Old Red Sandstone is a sedimentary rock which has weathered to create the smooth, rounded profiles, enlivened by ice-sculpted ridges and escarpments, which characterise much of the Brecon Beacons. More than half the Park is at an altitude of over 1,000ft (300m), much of this rising consistently to over 2,000ft (600m) to peak at just under 3,000ft (900m).

The highest peak is Pen y fan in the central Beacons, its distinctive table-topped summit standing at 2,907ft (886m). The borderland Black Mountains rise to an exposed 2,660ft (811m) at windy Waun Fach, while the Black Mountain's ghostly summit of Fan Brycheiniog looms out of the ever-present mist at an altitude of 2,630ft (802m). Forest Fawr, the high moorland consistently above 2,000ft (600m), is framed by Fan Fawr (2,409ft/734m) in the east and Fan Gyhirych (2,381ft/726m) in the west.

Haughty alpinists may scoff at the moderate height of these mountains. They do so at their peril. The Beacons have a formidable reputation for rewarding complacency by biting back. Gradual, deceptively gentle slopes lead

to knife-edge escarpments which plunge suddenly and steeply. The mountain-sides are treeless, affording scant protection from the chilling wind and few reference points for those not handy with a compass. And when mists and rain descend – as they often do – it is all too easy to become disorientated and hypothermic, as demonstrated by the number of victims which the Brecon Beacons continue to claim and the frequency with which the mountain rescue teams are called out. It is wise not to underestimate the challenges posed by the Special Air Service's favourite training ground.

The White Swan Inn at Llanfrynach, near Brecon

There is, though, a siren-like temptation to go out and walk these green hills and mountains. In the Brecon Beacons' case, there's more to it than the usual desire to escape the congested confines of the city. These uplands are inviting in a very special way which is, I think, all to do with one simple statistic: common land, which in this part of the world comes with *de facto* access, accounts for around 38 per cent of the Park's total area (or, to put it another way, there are 187sq miles' [484sq km] worth of open coun-tryside where you can roam to your heart's content).

The fact that this common land usually coincides with the most spectacular parts of the Park bestows upon the Brecon Beacons a special appeal for lovers of the Great Outdoors. A combination of the rounded, rolling moun-

Above: Walkers on the Sugar Loaf above Abergavenny (Harry Williams, courtesy of the National Trust)

Below: Maintenance work in the central Beacons (Harry Williams, courtesy of the National Trust)

tains typical of Old Red Sandstone and this wealth of common land has created an enviably 'open' landscape where the sense of freedom and endless space can sometimes be overwhelming. There are, in theory, limits to where you can and cannot walk on common land, a subject which is addressed in more detail later in this book. In practice, almost all of it is accessible (though there are occasional rights of way which must be adhered to) as long as farmers' interests are respected.

Long may it remain: after all, the freedom to roam over uncultivated mountain and moorland in a responsible way was one of the main aims behind the creation of the Park in the first place. Commercial companies have their mission statements; the Brecon Beacons National Park Authority has its vision statements. The following, taken from the National Park's Management Plan, sounds much better than the vacuous platitudes which preface the annual reports of many a multinational company: 'The vision is that these mountain commons and moorlands remain open, extensive and tranquil in character.'

Another passport to public access in the Brecon Beacons is land ownership. The National Park Authority owns around 14 per cent of land here, while the National Trust has acquired about 4 per cent (which includes the central massif around Pen y fan). The other major landowners in the Brecon Beacons are the Forestry Commission and Hyder (the company responsible for water and reservoirs). Most of the land (around two-thirds, which, of course, contains a significant element of common land) is in private ownership.

WATERFALL COUNTRY

Although the Brecon Beacons are synonymous with mountains, there is one corner of the National Park where the agoraphobic heights of Pen y fan can be swapped for a claustrophobic environment of caverns and narrow, wooded gorges. This is the one part of the Beacons that manages to spring a few scenic surprises. It's to be found along the southern rims of the Park where Old Red Sandstone gives way to a band of outcropping carboniferous limestone, a rock which weathers to create a craggy, fractured landscape of narrow gorges, pot holes, sink holes, caves and waterfalls.

The Brecon Beacons' so-called 'Waterfall Country' is centred around the isolated hamlet of Ystradfellte. Close by, along the Mellte and Hepste rivers, there's a series of spectacular waterfalls, including the famous Sgwd-yr-Eira ('The Spout of Snow') which overhangs to such a degree that walkers can follow a path behind the cascading falls without getting wet.

The area is, not surprisingly, popular with cavers. Just south of Ystradfellte, the giant mouth of Porth-yr-Ogof, possibly the largest cave entrance in Wales, swallows up the River Mellte. It's a favourite starting point for groups of well-equipped pot-holers keen to explore a labyrinthine underground maze created by the action of water on limestone. You don't have to be a skilled speleologist to experience the strange subterranean world along the southern rim of the Beacons. At the National Showcaves Centre for Wales at Dan-yr-Ogof, visitors have access to three separate cave systems, including the impressive 'Dome of St Paul's', a vast chamber 42ft (13m) high.

Abergavenny Castle, set beneath the Skirrid mountain

Ruined Llandovery Castle, on a steep mound

The National Showcaves Centre is the only large visitor attraction in the National Park. Like other indoor tourist attractions in Britain, it prays for rain (a plea answered with irksome regularity in these mountains), for precipitation is good for business. Tourist developments are sometimes a thorny issue in the National Park (it's inevitably a contentious subject; balancing the sometimes conflicting demands of conservation and recreation is never going to be an easy task).

Each National Park has to react differently to different local circumstances. It's fair to say, for example, that the Brecon Beacons – where large hotels and tourist attractions are conspicuous by their absence – is much further down the ladder in terms of tourism infrastructure than the Lake District. Whatever the rights and wrongs of the argument, no one should lose sight of the fact that the fundamental quality which draws 3.6 million people to the Brecon Beacons each year is all to do with the elemental appeal of exhilarating mountain landscapes.

An analysis of those 3.6 million reveals some interesting results. Two-thirds are day visitors, the remainder holidaymakers staying for one or more nights. So although the Brecon Beacons is easily accessible from London and the south east (and, along with the Peak District, the nearest bona fide mountains to the capital), the lion's share of visitors are locals from south Wales.

This may be something to do with perception. When Daniel Defoe came across the Beacons in 1724 he described them as 'horrid and frightful, even worse than those mountains abroad'. In Defoe's time, the romantic notion of landscape was yet to take hold. Nature was seen as a threat, not an inspiration. Yet the Beacons still suffer a little from the perception that they are perhaps too seriously mountainous, with few diversions for those who like their countryside to be a little gentler, a little more amenable.

ACTIVITIES FOR ALL

The truth is that there's a breadth of appeal in the Beacons that extends from the committed outdoor enthusiast to the visitors looking for an easy Sunday afternoon stroll. The Park's typecasting as a stark, mountainous area is true only up to a point. Yes, there are many challenges for the serious walker with plenty of experience (especially on the high ridges of the central Beacons and in the desolate wildernesses of the Black Mountain). But the Beacons also have their softer side, appreciated by casual walkers and families who prefer to follow easy, waymarked trails across common land or through the conifer forest on the lower-lying southern flank of the Park.

For mountain bikers, the Brecon Beacons are a seventh heaven, the UK's answer to the slickrock trails of Colorado. Pony trekkers appreciate the fact that these mountains are high enough to boast that you've been to the top but low enough for you to get there all the way on horseback. There are rivers in which to fish or canoe, and an idyllic inland waterway through the Usk valley

– the Monmouthshire and Brecon Canal – along which cruisers drift on a wooded shelf of land. On a rare stretch of low-lying flatland east of Brecon there's Llangorse Lake, the largest natural lake in south Wales; and along the southern reaches of the Park there are reservoirs – built to provide water to the nearby conurbations of south-east Wales – around which have developed a good range of leisure facilities.

Whatever your favourite outdoor pursuit, it's always possible to find a quiet, empty corner in which to pursue it. Avoid the obvious honeypots – which, in the main, means Storey Arms in the central Beacons and the busy route up Pen y fan – and you'll have the place to yourself.

Neither is it a particularly highly populated Park. Only 32,000 people live here, and there's only one town – Brecon – of note within the Park boundaries. Typical of the settlements are the villages strung out along the Usk valley – Crickhowell, Llangynidr, Sennybridge and the like – small places of around one to two thousand people. Brecon itself, population around 8,000, is an attractive place of narrow streets and Georgian houses. Centrally located more or less equidistant from the Park's eastern and western boundaries, it's a good base. There's a National Park Information Centre here; even better is the Park's Mountain Visitor Centre on Mynydd Illtud common a few miles away, which overlooks the highest peaks of the central Beacons and is worth visiting for the views alone. Visitors are well provided for in the Beacons: in addition to the facilities at Brecon and Mynydd Illtud there are eightteen information centres/agencies and a study centre.

Brecon is a busy place whose soul is still rooted in the soil. It continues to serve the local farming community, especially during the twice-weekly live-stock markets held here. But times are changing. From the look of the shops, pubs and hotels it's plain to see the contribution which tourism is now making to the local economy. Farmland and forest covers over 98 per cent of the land-mass of the Park. Agriculture dominates land use, but it gives full-time livelihoods to around only 1,500 of the Park's residents.

Culturally, there have been no great changes in recent times, no mass inva-sion of second-home owners or an overt Anglicisation of Welsh ways. This, one suspects, is because the Beacons is on a well-trodden path and is used to assimilating newcomers. The Normans colonised the Usk valley in medieval times; the A40, which follows the river, was an important stagecoach highway, opening up the area to traffic on the London to Fishguard route; in its wake, the new transients – the professionals working in the burgeoning white-collar industries of south-east Wales – have settled in places like Abergavenny and Crickhowell for the quality of life they can enjoy there while still being within easy commuting distance of their work in Cardiff or Newport.

Traditional Wales increases its grip the further west you travel. In Abergavenny, at the eastern gateway to the Park, a handful of people speak Welsh. By the time you reach Llandovery on the western approaches – a dis-tance of less than 40 miles (64km) along the A40 – 60 or 70 per cent are Welsh speakers.

In this part of Wales, the mountains do the real talking. The Brecon Beacons' solitudes, open spaces, boundless horizons and big skies reduce and refresh the individual; you are subservient to their moods, which can change alarmingly from balmy grass-scented summer to dank, boggy winter in an afternoon. Like no other part of Britain that I know, they put you in your place.

Pages 18–19: Pont Melin-fach on the River Neath in the Beacons' 'Waterfall Country'

1 The rocks beneath: geology and scenery

In my schooldays, I always felt a tinge of proprietorial pride when flicking through the pages of a geography text book and seeing the ice-sculpted lake of Llyn Cwm Llwch in the chapter on glaciation, or the sink holes and fractured pavements of Ystradfellte in the usually incomprehensible section which attempted to explain the effects of water on limestone. I'd been to these places, seen them for myself, and gradually – with the help of a patient geography master – I began to understand how landscapes were shaped.

I'm glad I persevered. It brought a new depth of appreciation to the way I looked at things which went beyond the superficial and the skin-deep. An understanding of why a valley has a certain shape, or how a waterfall is formed, adds an extra dimension to any encounter with the countryside. The Brecon Beacons is the most articulate of educators, reflecting geological features and forces with clarity and fluency. For my part, I'll try not to sound like a born-again teacher, though I will have to lay out a few basic principles in order to get to grips with the geology of these moors and mountains.

The title to this chapter may be a little misleading, for it doesn't quite reflect the fact that these mountains have achieved their shape for two reasons. Firstly, and fundamentally, there are 'the rocks beneath'. They will vary from place to place, producing different effects. But there's also a second element to be taken into consideration: the forces, mainly ice and water in the case of the Beacons, that have shaped, scooped and moulded the landscape over an immense period of time.

THE SANDSTONE BEDROCK

It's almost plain sailing in the Beacons as far as the first principle is concerned. There's a rare homogeneity to the landforms in the Brecon Beacons. Unlike the geological jumble of Snowdonia where an unfathomable mix of volcanic and sedimentary rocks come together to create a complex landscape, this is high country pure and simple, an uncomplicated place which springs few surprises. This uniformity is a reflection of the fact that most of the area – around two-thirds of the Park – is made up of the same rock, Old Red Sandstone, a sedimentary rock dating from the Devonian period of 395 to 345 million years ago, when it accumulated as gravels, sands and muds in the alluvial plains of large, meandering rivers. To this day, you can see in some rock surfaces on the summits of the Beacons ripple marks like those seen on sandy river beds.

The Old Red Sandstones give the Beacons their consistency of landscape, a quality captured in this nineteenth-century quote which talks about the 'softer charm of the Southern landscapes' (the Brecon Beacons), compared to the 'more rugged grandeur of the North' (a reference to Snowdonia). The soft,

The classic view of the Beacons from the A40 approaching Brecon, with Cribyn on the left and Pen y fan in the centre

On the Roman road above Trecastle

rounded profiles of the Beacons are indeed completely different to the jagged pinnacles and broken gullies of Snowdonia. Apart from one exception – a fierce, north-facing escarpment where the land dives downwards, suddenly losing hundreds of feet in height – there are no great accelerations or reversals in altitude.

Walk up the long, south-facing, dip slope of the central Beacons and you could be forgiven for thinking that you weren't climbing at all, so gradual is the gain in height. It's when you reach the top, and are approaching one of the Beacons' many razor-sharp ridges, that you have to be careful and remember that this high country isn't entirely predictable – especially when the summits are cloaked in a pervasive, disorienting mist. I have used the following description before when writing about the Beacons, but make no excuse for repeating it here, for it captures the essence of this graceful, green landscape. To me, the Beacons look like a petrified green sea, its mountains mirroring the peaks and troughs of an ocean, the gradual swell and sudden crash of waves cast in stone.

Of course, the deeper you delve, the more complicated things become. There are, in fact, at least five subdivisions of Old Red Sandstone in the Park, each one influencing the landscape in its own way: red marls on the fertile floor of the Vale of Usk and the lower slopes of the Black Mountains; the Senni beds exposed in the river valleys, like the Senni and Tarell, that flow northwards into the Usk; brownstones, consisting of red marls and brown sandstones which form much of the high ground in an east–west band across the Brecon Beacons; plateau beds, made up of conglomerates and coarse sandstones responsible for the distinctive 'table top' profiles of the Beacons' summits; and grey grits, quartz grits and sandstones, best seen between Bryniau Gleision (the 'Blue-Grey Hills' above the Talybont reservoir) and Penderyn.

But it's when you're out walking that the text book comes to life. The brownstones are the dominant sub-division of the Old Red Sandstones, largely responsible for the great north-facing scarp that forms the backbone of the Park. It runs from Bannau Sir Gaer, Fan Brycheiniog and Fan Hir (sometimes called the Carmarthen Fans) in the Black Mountain, across Fforest Fawr, through the central Beacons and on to the borderland Black Mountains. It's a hard, resistant rock made up of layer after layer, a wafer-like construction well over 1,000ft (300m) thick. You can see it exposed in a step-like series of bands in many

places along the escarpment – on Pen y fan's and Corn Du's slopes above Llyn Cwm Llwch, for example. Bannau Sir Gaer in the Black Mountain is another place where the steep staircase of brownstones is clearly exposed.

These brownstones are capped by the protective plateau beds, an even tougher rock which produces the flat-topped summits so characteristic of the Beacons.

Above and below: The broad Tarrell valley cuts into the Beacons south of Brecon

TABLE MOUNTAINS

The flat-topped summits of the Brecon Beacons are so distinctive that they are now used as logos and brands for tourism businesses. I live directly opposite a hill known locally as Table Mountain, the summit above Crickhowell that looks like a sloping football pitch. For mountaineers intent on reaching a definitive peak or pinnacle on which to plant a flag, the Beacons can be a frustrating place. Often the only way you really know you've reached the top is by looking for the trig point marking the indeterminate summit or hoping that the cairn, constructed by helpful fellow-walkers, is in the right place. So why don't the Beacons have Matterhorn-style peaks?

The highest layers of Old Red Sandstones in the Brecon Beacons are the tough brownstones and — above them — the even more resilient plateau beds. These horizontal or near-horizontal beds act as a protective cap or umbrella, producing the flattish summits, of which Pen y fan is the classic example.

The mountain road from Llwyn-onn reservoir to Penderyn

WHERE LIMESTONE MAKES AN APPEARANCE

While Old Red Sandstones reign supreme in these hills, to the south there is a very different landscape created by a very different rock. After the Devonian period came the Carboniferous, a geological era which began 345 million years ago and lasted for the next 65 million years. In the Beacons, these younger Carboniferous rocks meet the Old Red Sandstones along the southern fringes of the Park. Look at a cross-section of the geological structure of these uplands

On Mynydd Illtud common below the distinctive flat-topped summits of the central Beacons

and you will see the sandstones in the southern dip slope of the Beacons gradually sliding beneath younger rocks from the Carboniferous period.

The encounter between these two geological eras produces a profound change in landscape that cannot be over-emphasised. Suddenly, open moorland and smooth, bare-flanked mountain are replaced by craggy outcrops and narrow, deep gorges. Rural Wales rapidly loses its grip, threatened along the southern horizon by an encroachment of roads, towns, villages and evident reminders of an industrial past. This is the zone where the Beacons begin to decline, both physically and metaphorically, into somewhat unkempt, semi-urban surroundings.

The fact that the National Park ends – or begins, depending on your perspective – in this way is all down to the geology. The Carboniferous rocks that overlie the Old Red Sandstones are divided into three bands: carboniferous limestone, millstone grit and lower coal measures. Crucially, two of the three – limestone and coal – were key raw ingredients for the Industrial Revolution.

Within the Park itself there are only tiny pockets of outcropping coal - in small areas near Ystradgynlais and Coelbren, and east of Brynmawr in the Clydach gorge. The coal measures were exploited industrially in the mines of the south Wales valleys. Even deep in a mine there was an innate appreciation of the influences of geology. Directly beneath the rich seams of coal were the upper layers of millstone grit, known to colliers as the 'Farewell Rock' because when they reached it they knew there was no more of the 'black gold' to be mined economically. In the Park, this Farewell Rock is conspicuous on the Blorenge mountain above Abergavenny.

The most influential of the Carboniferous rocks in the Brecon Beacons is limestone which, along with millstone grit, outcrops in a band varying in width from 2 to 7 miles (3 to 11km), producing a classic karst landscape which, like other parts of the Beacons, crops up with regularity on the pages of geography text books.

The hamlet of Ystradfellte – no more than a church, pub and handful of houses – is at the centre of the Beacons' so-called 'Waterfall Country'. I first discovered it in the 1960s. By then, I had become quite familiar with the mountains of the central Beacons, and had heard intriguing stories of caves, pot holes and waterfalls you could walk behind without getting wet in the area around Ystradfellte. This unexplored corner of the Park (secret no longer, alas) was, I discovered, full of strange landforms. I came across rivers that suddenly disappeared underground, stumpy rock formations spread out across a craggy, irregular landscape, crazy-paving surfaces split by deep fissures, narrow, steep-sided gorges concealing gaping caverns and tiny passageways – and, at Sgwd-yr-Eira ('The Spout of Snow'), that previously mentioned curtain of water which I could view from inside out without a wetsuit. This was a very different Brecon Beacons to the one I'd been brought up with.

Many of these features, of great topographical interest, are created by the action of water on slowly soluble limestone rock. The most obvious manifestation of this is the exceptional number of major cave systems in the limestone belt, not just around Ystradfellte but in the Llangattock escarpment above Crickhowell and also in the upper Tawe valley. Experienced cavers will need no introduction to Porth yr Ogof, the huge cave entrance on the River Mellte

The giant cave entrance of Porth yr Ogof, near Ystradfellte

just south of Ystradfellte, or the vast cave systems – some of the largest in Britain – at Ogof Ffynnon Ddu, Abercraf and Ogof Agen Allwedd above Llangattock. This subterranean world of stalactites, stalagmites and weird and wonderful rock formations is open to all at the Dan yr Ogof National Showcaves Centre, Abercraf, where three separate caves – including the impressive, 70ft-high (21m) Cathedral Cave – are open to the public.

In the hills around Ystradfellte there's plentiful above-ground evidence of limestone in the form of numerous saucer- or funnel-like depressions known as swallow holes, sink holes or shake holes, where the rock below has, over the ages, dissolved. The bleak plateaux of Mynydd Llangynidr and Mynydd Llangattock above the Usk valley are pock-marked with countless shake holes – the largest concentration in Britain – caused in this case by the collapse of overlying millstone grit into the limestone caves below.

Then there's the case of the disappearing rivers. Porth yr Ogof, the largest cave entrance in Wales, swallows up the River Mellte which then flows underground for about a quarter of a mile before re-emerging downstream in a deep pool. Sometimes, the Mellte doesn't even make it as far as the cave mouth. In hot summers, the river disappears further upstream, leaving the riverbed on the approach to Porth yr Ogof dry as a bone. At times like this, the only evidence of the Mellte's existence is a ghostly one as the sound of it rushing underground is carried to the surface by pot holes.

The Neath is another river which performs a disappearing trick. At Pwll y Rhyd on its upper reaches the river pours into a spectacular steep-sided basin – a definitive swallow hole – before reappearing downstream at the White

Traditional field patterns bring order to the landscape in the hills flanking the Usk valley

Pages 28–9: An aqueduct carries the Monmouthshire and Brecon Canal across the waters of the Usk a few miles east of Brecon

Above: The dramatic limestone
escarpment above Llangattock not
only bears witness to industrial
activity, but is also important for its
natural history
Opposite: Abandoned quarries and
panoramic views from the only road
– the A4069 – to cross the Black
Mountain

Lady Cave. Like Porth yr Ogof in the neighbouring valley across the moor, it's
at its best in wet weather: in summer, the river has already disappeared beneath
the surface before reaching Pwll y Rhyd.

The ragged horizons in the southern Beacons, looking like rows of stumpy,
decayed teeth, are another manifestation of the underlying rock. These jagged
limestone cliffs or scars can be seen in places like Craig y Cilau on the
Llangattock escarpment and in the hills above the Dan yr Ogof Caves and
Craig-y-nos Country Park near Abercraf. From Craig y Cilau, you can look
northwards across the Usk valley to the oddity of Pen Cerrig-calch. At one
time, this 2,301ft-high (701m) peak would have been linked to the limestone
outcrops further south. Now, it is the sole remnant of the rock (*calch* is Welsh
for lime) marooned in a landscape dominated by sandstones.

Fascinating though these various landforms are, they cannot compete with
the one feature which has well and truly put this limestone country on the
map: its waterfalls. In geological terms, they are caused by the phenomenon of
differential erosion, when tougher, more water-resistant millstone grits come
into contact with softer rocks below. The falls are at their best on the Mellte
and Hepste rivers south of Ystradfellte. A riverside path leads from Porth yr
Ogof to a spectacular staircase of falls set in a beautiful wooded valley. First
comes Sgwd Clun-gwyn ('White Meadow Fall') followed by Sgwd Isaf Clun-
gwyn ('Lower White Meadow Fall') and Sgwd y Pannwr ('The Fall of the
Fuller'). The most famous of all is Sgwd yr Eira on the River Hepste, which
joins the Mellte downstream from Sgwd y Pannwr, its celebrity status no
doubt due to its acute overhang and the footpath which allows you to walk
underneath it with impunity.

While the Devonian and Carboniferous periods played a dominant role in shaping the Beacons, there are occasional geological manifestations from an even earlier era. The oldest rocks here, from Ordovician and Silurian times 500 to 395 million years ago, appear in the north-western edge of the Park, along the Tywi valley from Llandeilo to Llandovery. These rocks, named after the Celtic tribes known as the Ordovices and the Silures, accumulated gradually in shallowing seas and consist of mudstones, sandstones, shales and – occasionally – limestones.

THE FINAL POLISH

For the second instalment in the geological story of the Beacons we have to look beyond the 'rocks beneath' to the forces which gave them their final shape. The final polish to the Beacons' landscapes came during the Ice Age, which commenced about a million years ago and came to an end as recently as 10,000 to 12,000 years ago – in geological terms just a blink of an eyelid.

Wherever you look in these uplands you will see plentiful examples of the way in which glaciers have scooped and carved, modified and moulded their surroundings. The massive glaciers advanced slowly down valleys, icy behemoths eroding everything in their path. Some of the most classic features can be seen below the Beacons' north-facing ridges, where great amphitheatre-like hollows known as cwms, sometimes accompanied by lakes, have been gouged out of the mountains in a place where the ice accumulated at the head of the valley.

As the ice advanced it changed the profiles of valleys from a steep V-shape to a broader, more rounded, U-shape. The impact of the ice was a little subtler in the foothills of the southern Beacons. Here, the passage of the glaciers polished and planed the surfaces they passed across. Interestingly, the land-

WATER AND ICE

Cwm Llwch, the deep hollow beneath Corn Du and Pen y fan, is another of the Beacons' many textbook geological features. This cwm, or cirque, was caused by the relentless grinding and erosion of advancing glaciers during the Ice Age. The head of the valley that was once here was scooped out into its final shape by the ice. Cwm Llwch also contains another classic Ice Age feature – a glacial lake. As they crept forwards glaciers acted like giant snowploughs, building up mounds of debris in front of them. Gravel, boulders and other material were also carried within the body of the ice sheet itself. When the ice finally melted, this debris settled into the landscape forming mounds or moraines. In some cases – as at Cwm Llwch – the moraine acted as a dam, leading to the creation of a lake.

Llyn Cwm Llwch is one of a number of glacial lakes in the Beacons. Llyn y Fan Fach and Llyn y Fan Fawr are a pair of remote lakes beneath a steep escarpment in the Black Mountain crowned by the peak of Fan Brycheiniog. Llangorse Lake's glacial connections are not quite so self-evident. There are no ice-sculpted cwms soaring above this particular lake, which occupies a broad saucer of land well away from the ridges of the central Beacons. Nonetheless, its origins are glacial. When the ice retreated it deposited a moraine of bouldery gravel and clay here which led to an increase in the depth of waters that had collected in shallow glacial basin.

scape here sometimes reveals the direction in which the ice travelled, for it is etched as scratch or striation marks on the rocks (there are good examples of this on the millstone grit around Ystradfellte).

The ice also carried sandstone boulders considerable distances – some from the Beacons were transported and dumped as far away as the Vale of Glamorgan. This depositional role exemplifies the second effect which glaciers have on the landscape. As well as eroding they also picked up and carried material – soil, rock fragments and debris, known collectively as glacial drift – which was subsequently deposited across the landscape when the ice retreated. One of the most obvious examples of this is the mound, or moraine, which in some cases led to the creation of a glacial lake.

Over the ages, these moraines blended into the landscape, making them difficult to spot without a tutored eye. There's a particularly large example near the village of Llanfihangel Crucorney north of Abergavenny, which had a dramatic effect on the course of a local river. The River Honddu flows southwards through the Vale of Ewyas. Originally, it would have continued south to Abergavenny, but now abruptly alters its course when it encounters the moraine near Llanfihangel Crucorney which steers it north eastwards.

Immediately after the end of the Ice Age, the Beacons experienced prolonged freeze-thaw conditions. Much of the clayey drift was washed down valley slopes forming rounded projections and terraces. These were in turn cut into by rivers and streams carrying fine-grained soil further downstream, creating the fertile lower reaches of valleys like the Usk. In the wet, poorly drained high country, there's nowadays a peaty, acidic landscape – in agricultural terms a marginal environment – which just about supports hill-sheep farming.

The process of change goes on, usually imperceptibly. In recent years, however, the Beacons have experienced some bizarre weather. The false promise of early springtime has been followed by snow at Easter. Recent autumns and winters have been amongst the wettest on record. Is it global warming, or just the start of another natural weather cycle? Whatever the answer, it is part of an ongoing process that is still shaping the Beacons.

There's a breathtaking view of the sheltered Usk valley from the summit of Tor y Foel above Llangynidr

2 Climate, vegetation and wildlife

Above and right: Snow regularly clothes the high peaks of the Beacons in winter

Daniel Defoe, author of *Robinson Crusoe*, must have preferred desert islands to highlands. His impression of the Beacons as being 'horrid and frightful' was based on a trip to south Wales in 1724. Allowing for the fact that mountains weren't particularly fashionable in the pre-Wordsworthian era, I know how he must have felt. When the sun is out and the grass is green, there's no finer nor fresher place to be than in the high Beacons. When it's raining, misty and blowing a gale, and the land underfoot resembles a dank, matted sponge, desert islands don't seem so bad after all.

Rain and the Welsh hills are synonymous. The high ground in the Park can have as much as 100in (250cm) of rain a year coming across in wave after wave of westerly fronts, though there are other parts of the Beacons – in rain shadow areas lying east of the high ground, such as the middle Usk valley – where that figure can be cut by two-thirds.

Welsh weather is a bit of a lottery at the best of times. In the Beacons, the

odds are even higher than in other parts of the country. When the sun is shining in Crickhowell, just 10 miles (16km) away on the peak of Pen y fan you can be subjected to a truly 'horrid and frightful' experience if you're caught without fleeces and waterproofs. Even the locals can become bamboozled by the Beacons' alarming mood swings. Last year, I climbed the Sugar Loaf mountain on an August day, setting off from a bright and balmy Abergavenny, only to arrive at the top seriously chilled by a biting wind.

Neither can you rely on the seasons. Winter disappears prematurely, only to arrive again with a vengeance in early spring. Summer never seems properly to establish itself, while autumn is an unpredictable hotch-potch of sun and showers. I don't want to hark back to the 'blue remembered hills' of boyhood when summer was summer and winter was winter, but is it just me who thinks that our climate has lost its resolute seasonality?

The Park's flora also has the capacity to spring a few surprises. There's a complexity to the pattern of its distribution, the result of local variations in soil and rocks, aspect and altitude. To the untrained eye, it's a complexity which is not immediately apparent. The consistency of landscape in the Beacons, a subject touched on in previous chapters, leads to an impression of uniformity of plantlife. Stand on any high ground and it seems as if the coarse matting of grassland and moorland rolls on forever, blanketing the land to the exclusion

of everything else. Impressions are deceptive, for there's a surprising variety of flora to be found here – no less than 850 species of flowering plants are indigenous to the Park, including some extremely rare botanic jewels.

The bare expanses of highland we see today are a relatively recent phenomenon. Until about 6,000 years ago, the upper reaches of the Beacons may well have been forested to 2,000ft (600m). A change in climate and the attentions of our tree-chopping ancestors conspired to lower the tree line to about 1,000ft (300m), laying the foundations for the vegetation cover in the higher ground that has since developed.

This is an opportune time to correct, once and for all, the misunderstanding surrounding Fforest Fawr, the 'Great Forest', one of the four major upland areas in the Park. It might well have been a woodland in prehistoric times, though this has nothing to do with its name. It was called Fforest Fawr in the Middle Ages, when the term 'forest' was used to describe a hunting ground. By then, it would have been the treeless expanse of moor we see today (though in relatively recent times there has been some commercial conifer planting).

Above: Cray reservoir south west of Sennybridge
Right: The high moors of Fforest Fawr, one of the Park's four mountain ranges

ICE AGE SURVIVORS

The cool, shady crags of Craig Cerrig-gleisiad in the north-eastern corner of Fforest Fawr provide a habitat for rare arctic-alpine plants like purple saxifrage and roseroot. These tenacious leftovers from the end of the Ice Age 10,000 years ago are at their southernmost limit in Britain in the glacier-gouged north- and east-facing scarps of the Beacons, not just at Craig Cerrig-gleisiad but on slopes from the Carmarthen Fans in the Black Mountain across to the central Beacons.

The special chemistry of the rocks has assisted their survival. These mountains consist largely of sandstones, a rock which typically produces acidic, limeless soils, unloved by many alpines. On the scarps, a change in the geology — brought about by the presence of lime-rich brownstones from the Old Red Sandstone series — results in soil which is sufficiently limey to allow a varied range of alpines and arctic-alpines to flourish. Although obviously suited to their environment, their survival must also be due to the fact that they are tucked away on inaccessible ledges and steep gullies, protected from the attentions of voracious mountain sheep.

In the Black Mountain

RARE ARCTIC-ALPINES

Fforest Fawr is the unlikely home to some of those aforementioned botanic 'jewels'. In the far north east, its bleak moors give way to the dark crags and hidden hillsides of Craig Cerrig-gleisiad, a National Nature Reserve which contains extremely rare arctic-alpine plants. The 156-acre (63ha) reserve not only reveals rarities but also gives us an insight into the Beacons' unexpectedly diverse plantlife. Over 500 different plants colonise its rocky outcrops, gullies, bogs, pools and streams.

The rich plantlife along Craig Cerrig-gleisiad and other glacial scarps in the Beacons has another explanation, because they serve as a meeting place for highland and lowland flora. Among the arctic-alpines and alpines you will also see plants usually associated with lowlands – primroses, cowslips, early purple orchids, wood anemones and so on – which have crept up the contours to colonise higher ground. In places where lime-rich soils give way to a more acidic habitat, heathers, sheep's fescue and bilberry add yet more variety.

These three species serve as an introduction to the acidic high country that unfurls from the scarps, a harsh environment that is not without its diversity of plantlife. The moors and mountains are, in fact, made up of a mosaic of different plants which form their own colonies. Walkers will be only too familiar with the terrain. As they trudge upwards, grass and heathland gradually degenerate into an ankle-breaking expanse of tufty moorland and boot-soaking bogland. In the saturated, badly-drained blanket bog, sphagnum mosses are the dominant plants. In these acidic moors you might catch sight of small touches of alternative colours amongst the dominant browns, auburns and

Above: The Gospel Pass above Hay-on-Wye is the highest road in south Wales
Right: Heather, a common sight in the Beacons' high country

mottled greens, indicating the occasional presence of flowering plants such as heath bedstraw, tormentil and heath milkwort.

Other plants that happily survive in this peaty high country include heather, bilberry, fescue, mat grass and purple moorgrass. The latter is especially prevalent along the poorly-drained dip slopes of the central Beacons, Fforest Fawr and the Black Mountain. In other western areas where it's just as wet but better drained, sheep's fescue and mat grass – plants which prefer drier soils – cover the moors. As precipitation declines further east in the Park along the borderland Black Mountains, heather and bilberry moorlands – characteristic of places with lower rainfall – become more commonplace.

MORE RARITIES IN LIMESTONE COUNTRY

The carboniferous limestone country along the southern rim of the Park produces yet more changes in the flora. In the Penmoelallt outcrops above the Taff Fawr valley north of Merthyr Tydfil, there's a covering of oak and ash, a woodland fast disappearing from Wales. Particularly characteristic of limestones are yew and whitebeam trees, the latter a relative of the mountain ash. One species of whitebeam at Penmoelallt (a 17-acre/7ha Forest Nature Reserve) has a very special status. Ley's whitebeam is unique. It cannot be found anywhere else in the world apart from one other location across the valley.

Penmoelallt is one of a number of nature reserves along the limestone belt which owe their designation largely to their valuable plantlife. At Brynmawr,

Despite an industrial past, the Clydach gorge is noted for its woodland cover

the Park boundary makes a point of crossing the A465 'Heads of the Valleys' road – the dividing line between rural and industrial south Wales – to enclose the Clydach gorge, a site renowned for its odd combination of industrial heritage and outstanding mature woodlands. The 55-acre (22ha) Cwm Clydach National Nature Reserve is cloaked by native beechwoods, a tree rare in Wales. Where light does manage to penetrate this heavy canopy, look out for occasional plants such as the rare soft-leaved sedge, the unusual bird's nest orchid, early dog violet and wild thyme.

There are more beechwoods close by at the 157-acre (64ha)

The nature reserve at Carreg Cennen
Castle combines influences of Old
Red Sandstone and limestone

Craig y Cilau reserve on the escarpment above Llangattock in the Usk valley. In addition to an exceptional cave system (see Chapter 1), Craig y Cilau is noted for the variety of its trees, which include rare whitebeams and the extremely rare lesser whitebeam. There are more caves at the 1,021-acre (413ha) Ogof Ffynnon-ddu reserve in the upper Tawe valley near Abercraf. Botanic interest here focuses on small areas of limestone grassland which supports plants such as limestone bedstraw and mountain everlasting, together with specialities like mountain melick, lesser meadow rue and lily of the valley, which grow in crevices in the limestone pavement. Overlooked by Carreg Cennen Castle in the far west of the National Park is Coed y Castell (the 'Wood of the Castle'), a 39-acre (16ha) reserve with a mixed habitat where the Beacons' two main geological constituents appear together. In the west of the reserve there is carboniferous limestone with a typical covering of ash, next to the Old Red Sandstone in the east, which is covered by oak and bracken.

The limestone gorges of 'Waterfall Country' around Ystradfellte are also of considerable interest. Among the ashes you will see a variety of ferns, while this fractured, inaccessible terrain is also home to surviving pockets of native broadleaved woodland – oak, birch and alder – remnants of the thick forests which once covered much of the Beacons.

Broadleaved woodland nowadays covers an extremely modest portion of the Park – around 12,500 acres (5,000ha), representing less than 4 per cent of the total area. But there are other trees here which are spread across 30,000 acres (12,000ha), almost one-tenth of the Park. These are the commercial conifer forests, ranged in a broad semi-circle around the central Beacons and growing on poor land which, were it used for farming, would offer low productivity. Among the conifers, Japanese and hybrid larch and Norway spruce (the Christmas tree) are common. But most common of all is the fast-growing Sitka spruce, originally from the West Coast of America, which thrives in a wet, cool climate and at an altitude of up to and beyond 1,400ft (425m) where most other trees would struggle to survive.

Above: Dyffryn Crawnon, a remote side valley off the Usk at Llangynidr
Right: The red kite has spread into the central Beacons from the Cambrian Mountains

BIRDLIFE IN THE PARK

The woodlands of the Brecon Beacons are one of a number of distinctive habitats, each of which is favoured by different species of birds. It is, of course, far too simplistic to create a rule which says that certain birds can only be found in certain habitats. But in terms of broad guidelines, birds do have preferred habitats; and the variety of the latter in the Beacons, a mix of lowland and highland, farmland and moorland, wood and water, leads to a rewarding spread of species. There are over 200 different kinds of bird in the Park, of which about 100 breed here. And the Beacons' bird populations are quite plentiful, especially in lowland areas.

The habitats break down into four broad categories, based on their distinctive vegetation: woodland, upland, farmland and water (lakes, reservoirs and rivers). The Park's deciduous woodlands attract more birds than the conifer plantations because of their wider opportunities for feeding and nesting. Over thirty species breed here, the most notable of which are redstarts, wood warblers, pied flycatchers and tree pipits, all summer migrants. Nuthatches and treecreepers are not great travellers, remaining faithful to these woods throughout the year. They can be seen not only perched or flying but also climbing trees.

Even in the gloomy monoculture of the conifer forest there is an interesting birdlife. Tree pipits are partial to conifers as well as deciduous forest. Whinchats can often be seen perched on top of small conifers, though the reclusive grasshopper warbler is more often heard than seen. Among the close-planted ranks of Sitka spruces in the really thick forest, you will look long and hard for birdlife, though even these dark, impenetrable glades attract one or

two species such as the coal tit, a small bird, and the even smaller goldcrest.

The uplands in the Beacons are a place of little shelter and high rainfall. There is a general uniformity of conditions here which leads to a correspondingly limited variety of birdlife in comparison to the Park's other main habitats. Two common sights which can be seen circling in the skies are the buzzard and raven, both large birds of prey. Another, the kestrel, can be seen searching for food in farmland and well as moorland.

But pride of place must go to the majestic red kite, a rare raptor which is slowly making a comeback in these hills and mountains – especially in the west of the Park – after facing extinction. You can also count yourself lucky if you spot the peregrine falcon, another rare bird of prey. One of the best places to catch sight of peregrine is at Craig Cerrig-gleisiad, where the crags provide a safe nesting place for many birds.

The red grouse is another upland rarity. At one time, the Brecon Beacons had its own Scottish-style grouse moors, around Llangattock and Blaenavon in the south. Some birds, the remnants of the most southerly indigenous population in Britain, can still be seen on the heather moors in the south east of the Park, a habitat which also attracts merlins.

Of the smaller upland birds, the two most common species are the meadow pipit and skylark, the most numerous breeding birds in these parts. Wheatears nest among boulders or stone walls, while ring ouzels similarly favour rocky outcrops and gullies. Both are migrants, so can only be seen in spring and summer. In summer and autumn, look out too for lapwing, commonly seen in large flocks.

The pattern of farming in the National Park, where stock is reared in small fields bordered by hedgerows and a scattering of trees, provides a good nesting and feeding habitat for many birds. Carrion crows, rooks, jackdaws and the conspicuous black-and-white magpie are all commonplace. Another common farmland bird is the bullfinch, often seen among the hedgerows or hunting the fields for food along with other finches like the chaffinch, greenfinch and goldfinch. Other birds of the hedgerow include the yellowhammer and hedge sparrow.

THE RETURN OF THE KITE

Not so long ago, the majestic red kite was faced with extinction in Britain, its numbers down to only a handful of pairs struggling to survive in the remoter parts of central Wales. Through encouragement and protection, the kite has made a comeback and can now be seen again in the skies of central Wales and parts of the Brecon Beacons – so much so that the area enjoys a new identity as 'Kite Country'. The strikingly coloured bird of prey, with its chestnut-red body, contrasting white patches under its wings and a pale grey head, has a wingspan of around 5½ft (nearly 2m) and a distinctive forked tail.

The environmentally-inspired Kite Country project has been set up to encourage visitors to the area and help them see the bird. Individual sightings are now becoming more common – it's an unforgettable spectacle if you're fortunate enough to see two or three pairs wheeling in the skies or performing agile aerobatics.

If you want more than a brief glimpse you should visit one of the network of Kite Country Centres specially established to make the bird as easy to see as possible. Not only does kite feeding take place at most of these centres, but they also provide a wealth of information on scenic walks and local wildlife in general. The centres are located in mid Wales (the nearest to the Brecon Beacons is Gigrin Farm at Rhayader). Closer to home, but on a smaller scale, there are also Kite Country Information Points – the nearest are at Llandovery, Llyn Llech Owain Country Park near Llandeilo, and Llanwrtyd Wells.

Birds don't discriminate against the relative newcomer – and a man-made one at that – of Talybont reservoir, just 4 miles (6.4km) from Llangorse. Pochard, tufted duck, mallard and teal are among the many species which happily take to Talybont's waters at any time of the year, though like nearby Llangorse the numbers of different species are at their largest when the winter migrants arrive. Talybont's role as a refuge for birdlife was formally recognised in 1975 when it was made a local nature reserve covering 490 acres (198ha), most of which is water.

Other aquatic birds associated with the Beacons include the kingfisher, a species which particularly favours the wooded banks of the Monmouthshire and Brecon Canal, moorhen, water rail and common sandpiper.

Apart from the street-wise sheep who hang around certain popular car parks, ready to muscle in as soon as anyone appears with anything edible, you won't be intimidated by the Beacons' four-legged wildlife. Bears and wolves have long gone, leaving the fox, badger and otter as the largest wild mammals remaining in the Park. Badgers are quite common, though the beleaguered otter, suffering from the problems of water pollution and the destruction of riverbank habitats, has declined. On the other hand, the polecat – its smaller relative – has increased in numbers, possibly because it has been freed from persecution thanks to the decline in gamekeeping.

Rabbits, hares, stoats and weasels are common – the first couple are too common if, like me, you try to cultivate a garden next to an open field. As in other parts of Britain, you'll see the immigrant – and dominant – grey squirrel everywhere, but look in vain for the native red squirrel.

Wild ponies enjoy the open moorlands of Fforest Fawr

3 Man's influence

The bare and empty solitudes of the Brecon Beacons appear, on first acquaintance, to be bereft of history. You can look long and hard to find the footprint of man among the moors of the central Beacons or the wildernesses of the Black Mountain.

Yet from the earliest times, the Beacons have been settled, colonised, conquered and farmed. They have been exposed to the influences of prehistoric man, Roman soldiers, early Celtic-Christian missionaries, native princes, Norman conquerors and even industrial innovators; it's just that the evidence is not immediately apparent. It's tucked away in hidden corners and quiet valleys, in farmers' fields and on mountain summits – which makes its discovery all the more rewarding.

It's also a case of quality triumphing over quantity. The way in which the past reveals itself in the Beacons is best summed up by its castles. Wales is often billed as a 'land of castles'. Hundreds of medieval strongholds – experts are still arguing over the precise figure – dot the landscape. In the north, they seem to appear over almost every hill. In the Beacons, you need to know where to look.

But when you find Carreg Cennen, you'll know you are in the presence of an historic superstar. For many – myself included – it's the ultimate Welsh castle, surpassing by far the more famous fortresses of Caernarfon and Conwy built by King Edward I on the north Wales coast. Perched on a limestone crag in a remote corner of the Black Mountain, Carreg Cennen still retains an authentic air of medieval times. Up there, in the weatherbeaten eagle's nest with low cloud spilling off the empty moors, it's not difficult to cast your mind back 600 years to the time when Owain Glyndŵr and his men stormed the castle during the last Welsh uprising.

PREHISTORIC BEGINNINGS

You can reach back many thousands of years in the Beacons, to the time of megalithic monuments, burial chambers and stone circles. As with Carreg Cennen, these mountains for the most part keep their best prehistoric sites well hidden. In around 12,000BC, the glaciers that affected this part of Wales began to melt. In the post-

Carreg Cennen Castle, spectacularly located on a limestone outcrop near Trapp

HOUSES OF THE DEAD

The construction of large burial chambers must have represented a huge challenge to Neolithic communities. In the Beacons, where slab stone was plentiful, the internal structure of the tomb would have consisted of uprights and capstones, a framework covered with an earthen mound (in other parts of Britain, where suitable stones were scarce, the tombs would have been built entirely of earth). The shifting of 50-ton slabs of rock must have involved considerable ingenuity and organisation. Excavation at the Gwernvale tomb near Crickhowell has revealed evidence not just of communal burial but also of local farming activity in the form of stones for grinding corn, fragments of animal bone (including domesticated cattle, sheep and pigs) and flint tools such as axes, knives and scrapers.

Right: The Gwernvale prehistoric tomb on the outskirts of Crickhowell
Opposite: An ancient waymark or place of ritual? Maen Llia is easily spotted amongst the bare moors of Fforest Fawr

glacial period, Palaeolithic (Old Stone Age) hunters may have wandered through the tundra and forest, stalking deer and ox. But for the first hard evidence of settlement we have to look to Neolithic (New Stone Age) times.

From around 5000BC, man's influence began to impact on the landscape. Our Neolithic ancestors were Britain's first farmers: they began to control their environment as opposed to being dictated to by the forces of nature, initiating a conversation between man and nature which continues to shape and modify this planet – for better or worse – to this day. Neolithic farmers attacked the thick forests which covered the land below 2,000ft (600m), probably using the land for a combination of crops and animals.

One of the few sites from these distant times which is easily accessible is the Gwernvale ancient tomb, a collection of large stones located beside the A40 road on the northern outskirts of Crickhowell at the entrance to the Manor Hotel. This is the remnant of a chamber used for the communal burial of the dead. What we now see are the bare bones of a tomb that would originally have been covered with an earth mound.

Other major prehistoric sites are in more obscure locations. Their siting may well be linked to their original purpose. Go up into the featureless expanses of Fforest Fawr, where mile after mile of moorland rolls away into the far distance. It's a bare landscape which can be somewhat disorienting, so the eye is easily drawn to the few lone standing stones which prick the horizon. These enigmatic monuments, dating from the late Neolithic/early Bronze Age of about 2400 to 1800BC, are shrouded in mystery. They may have originally been erected as landmarks or route markers, pointing the way across these trackless moors. Other theories suggest that they may have served as territorial markers or statues to the gods.

The most impressive is Maen Llia, a massive monolith standing 12ft (3.7m) tall at the head of the Llia valley between Ystradfellte and Sennybridge. Maen Llwyd, at the head of the Grwyne Fechan valley in the Black Mountains, is even more remote. Located on the flanks of Gadair Fawr at an altitude of

1,880ft (573m), it is believed to be the highest standing stone in south Wales.

There are around thirty such stones scattered across the National Park, mainly in the uplands around the Tawe valley and along the Vale of Usk. Their survival through the ages may be due to the mystery and superstition which surrounded them, prompting an ancient Welsh law which carried the penalty of death to anyone found harming the stones.

The standing stones were probably erected by the Bronze Age Beaker Folk, so-called because of the shape of their pottery. These new colonists arrived in the Beacons in about 2000BC during a time when the climate became warmer and drier. They also created stone circles and alignments – but again, mystery shrouds their purpose. Archaeologist Sir Mortimer Wheeler believed that they were the focal point of secular and religious affairs in a time when 'the two were still essentially one and indivisible'. More recent speculation, echoing those surrounding Stonehenge, suggest that they served as giant calendars, keeping track of the sun, moon and stars.

One of my favourite ancient monuments – which I stumbled across completely by accident after a piece of myopic map reading when attempting foolishly to traverse the Black Mountain by bike – is Saith Maen, an alignment of seven stones on moorland high above the Craig y nos Country Park in the upper Tawe valley. Interestingly, the alignment – not a common feature in Wales – points in the direction of Cerrig Duon, a circle of twenty stones (it's actually egg-shaped, a rarity in Britain). This ancient site stands at 1,270ft (387m) near the source of the Tawe on the eastern flank of the Black Mountain, accompanied by a large standing stone known as Maen Mawr just outside the circle. Is it pure coincidence that Saith Maen points to Cerrig Duon, 3 miles (4.8km) away across the mountain? Only the Beaker Folk would have the answer.

CELTIC HILLFORTS

You don't need accurate map-reading skills to discover evidence of the next wave of settlers to these parts, though a good pair of walking boots and plenty of stamina are *de rigueur*. Cast your eyes to the mountains and there's a reasonable chance that you'll be looking at one of the twenty-odd Iron Age hillforts in the Park. Many a prominent hilltop in the Beacons displays features which are quite obviously man-made: ditches, embankments, ramparts, unnatural-looking piles of stone and so on. Again, there is no definitive explanation for the siting and purpose of such settlements. Were they permanently inhabited strongholds or just used at times of threat? Perhaps they served no bellicose role at all, especially since the customs of their builders could point to their entirely peaceful use as farming or trading centres.

Many of these hillforts date from around 600BC, marking a transition from the Bronze to Iron Age as Celtic settlers from Europe brought with them new skills in iron-making and farming – and, according to many, a whole new culture which still informs and inspires Wales and the Welsh. A definite pattern of cultivation was introduced, with the clearance of forests, the farming of the lower, more fertile ground, and the grazing of livestock on the higher land around the hillfort.

When I gaze out of the window of my house I look across the Usk valley to Crug Hywel, Howell's Fort. This table-topped hillfort stands at 1,480ft (451m) above the little town of Crickhowell (you don't need to be good at anagrams to work out the etymology of this particular place name). It's a typical example, being of moderate height and overlooking good agricultural land, with a commanding location and strong natural defences. So perhaps Crug Hywel served merely as a meeting place and trading centre for outlying farms, an Iron Age equivalent of the role nowadays played by the market town of Brecon. This speculation shifts to firmer ground in the light of the following expert opinion: 'Nor is there evidence that hillforts [in the Brecon Beacons] were the scene of serious assault, still less of sieges.'

Whatever their purpose, they are mightily inspiring places. It's difficult to believe that Castell Dinas, north-west of Crickhowell, was built for anything other than defensive motives. Standing aggressively at the head of the Rhiangell valley, it guards a strategic gap in the mountains now breached by the A479 to Talgarth. Strangely, its well-preserved Iron Age ditches and ramparts have weathered better than the masonry which was added to this site by medieval castle builders, who readily exploited its military value.

The finest hillfort in the Beacons is undoubtedly Carn Goch in the foothills of the Black Mountain near Llangadog. One of the largest hillforts on Wales, it covers 30 acres (12ha) of hillside. You don't need the finesse of an archaeologist's eye to appreciate Carn Goch: its massive defences are plain to see in the shape of gateways, ditches and great mounds of stone rubble.

Carn Goch in the Black Mountain, the largest Iron Age hillfort in south Wales

THE ARRIVAL OF THE ROMANS

Many of these hillforts, occupied by a belligerent Celtic tribe known as the Silures, were still in use when the Romans turned their attentions to Wales not long after arriving in Britain in AD43. The lowland coastal strip didn't impede the progress of the sophisticated Roman machine, though it took a little longer to make inroads into mountainous south Wales.

But conquest was inevitable and the Silures were soon subdued. Roads were laid down, camps and forts were constructed. Central to the Romans' presence in the Beacons was Y Gaer (it simply means 'The Fort') near Brecon, built to accommodate 500 cavalry. This rectangular stronghold, which today stands unceremoniously – and almost forgotten – in farmland beside the confluence of the Usk and Yscir rivers, dates from around AD80. Originally built of earth and timber, it was reconstructed in stone about sixty years later. Well-preserved stretches of wall and gateway were revealed during excavations in the 1920s.

Another compelling, hidden spot dating from Roman times is Y Pigwn on the bleak moors surrounding the Usk reservoir. Irregular lumps and bumps in the landscape are all that remain of a temporary camp established by the Romans during their early campaigns. This marching camp would have been thrown up, possibly overnight, as protection against the Silures.

Reference to marching leads on to what are some of the great glories of the Beacons – its Roman roads. Y Pigwn stands beside a stretch of road that forges its single-minded way across the moor, connecting Y Gaer with another Roman fort at Llandovery. An unwavering, as-the-crow-flies route, which sticks to strategic, easily defended high ground, it displays all the classic features of Roman engineering. It's a wonderful walking route, with magnificent views south to the brooding Black Mountain and north to the rolling farmlands and forests that clothe the foothills of the Cambrian Mountains. When the topography forces the route to abandon its secure high country west of Y Pigwn, there's more evidence of Roman ingenuity in the way in which skilfully constructed bends zigzag downwards.

Another classic Roman route through the Beacons is Sarn Helen, which linked Y Gaer with the Roman fort of Nidum (at Neath). You can pick it up at Coelbren on the southern fringes of the Brecon Beacons and follow it north eastwards through Fforest Fawr more or less all the way to the National Park's Visitor Centre on Mynydd Illtud. Just after the track crosses the River Neath there's a conspicuous landmark standing all alone on an exposed, windy crest. This is the slender pillar of Maen Madoc, a 9ft-high (2.7m) stone with a plaintive inscription in Latin dating from Roman times: '(The stone) of Dervacus, son of Justus. He lies here'.

*Left: The Roman road above Trecastle illustrates the way in which the Romans preferred to keep to high ground for strategic reasons
Below: Y Gaer, near Brecon, was once an important Roman base*

There's still some uncertainty about the other 'Roman' road in the Beacons. This is the so-called Gap route, possibly built as a north–south link connecting the Roman camp at Penydarren, Merthyr Tydfil with Y Gaer, which cuts through the central Beacons by exploiting a deep dip in the ridge.

ILLTUD'S COMMON

The National Park's Visitor Centre is located on Mynydd Illtud, the grassy common overlooking Pen y fan. The common is named after St Illtud, a Celtic religious missionary who was as influential in spreading the Christian message in Wales was St David, the patron saint. According to legend, he lies buried on the common at Bedd Illtud, a site near the road just north of the Visitor Centre marked by a collection of large stones in a shallow hollow. Until 1995, a derelict church dedicated to Illtud – now demolished – stood by the farm on the north-western approach to the Visitor Centre. One theory suggests that Illtud established a hermitage here and that it remained a site of Christian worship from that time until the 1920s. There is even the suggestion that it has pagan, pre-Christian roots.

Y Gaer remained in service as a military base until around AD200, and may again have been used from AD300 as a civilian settlement. By AD400, the Romans were in retreat, their empire in ruins. It's unlikely that their grip in the hostile high country of south Wales was ever as tenacious as it was in the more amenable lowlands. There's little evidence of attempts to establish townships in the Beacons, though we know that there was a villa at Llanfrynach and that dwellings sprung up around Y Gaer. For hard evidence of their occupation, go to the Brecknock Museum in Brecon, which contains excellent displays of Roman artefacts including pottery, carved stones and coins.

After the departure of the Romans, Britain was plunged into a Dark Age. It was an era illuminated only by the emergence of the early Christian church, a movement led by dynamic fifth- and sixth-century missionaries like St Illtud and St David. From his monastic settlement in Pembrokeshire David, or Dewi Sant, travelled far and wide: the medieval priory at Llanthony in the remote Vale of Ewyas stands on the site of a sixth-century chapel dedicated to him (Llanthony's name is a corruption of the Welsh *Llanddewi nant honddu*, meaning 'The Church of St David on the River Honddu').

There's a scattering of religious sites with truly ancient, Celtic-Christian roots throughout the Brecon Beacons. Take any place beginning with *llan* (meaning 'church of') and there's a good chance that its lineage may go back 1,500 years. Llangorse's Church of St Paulinus, dedicated to David's tutor, originates from a monastic community founded by Paulinus in the sixth century. The far-flung hamlet of Llanddeusant lost in the foothills of the Black Mountain grew up around another church with monastic links to Paulinus. At Llanddew near Brecon, the Church of St David was first mentioned as a religious site in the early sixth century, while Llangattock's Church of St Catwg is named after a contemporary of David.

The Dark Ages, characterised by uncertainty and turmoil, did at least produce one certainty – the emergence, for the first time, of an official border between Wales and England, a barrier which reinforced a separate Welsh identity. Tenth-century Saxon law stated in no uncertain terms that 'neither shall a Welshman cross into English land nor an Englishman cross into Welsh land without the appointed man from that other land who should meet him at the bank and bring him back again without any offence being committed'.

The 'bank' was Offa's Dyke, a massive earthwork built by Offa, ruler of the Midland kingdom of Mercia, in the eighth century. Up to 20ft (6m) high in places, it ran from Prestatyn on the north Wales coast to Chepstow in the south, a distance of 142 miles (228km). In the Brecon Beacons, the line of this ancient border can be followed by walking the section of the Offa's Dyke Path on the ridge above the Vale of Ewyas.

CONTROL THROUGH CASTLE-BUILDING

The force of the Norman Conquest of Britain in 1066, was, like that of the Roman invasion a millennium earlier, diluted somewhat when it reached mountainous Wales. Nonetheless, in lowland areas like the Usk valley rough-and-ready motte-and-bailey castles built of earth and timber were hastily thrown up to control strategic routes and to contain the native inhabitants. In geographic terms, the Norman lordships were divided into two parts: the favoured, more fertile lowlands known as the Englishry, and the uplands of the Welshry where native chieftains still ruled, albeit under the wary eye of the Normans.

Neither was there any great agricultural revolution in the rugged hill country. As long as rents were paid, the native Welsh were left largely to their own

Above: The Offa's Dyke Path runs along the border from north to south Wales, following wherever possible the line of the ancient earthen barrier (Wales Tourist Board)
Left: Mynydd Illtud is named after an influential early Christian saint

BRECON'S BEGINNINGS

The name Brecon can be traced back to the so-called Dark Ages and the powerful Welsh chieftain Brychan. Breconshire, or its old county title of Brecknock, derives from Brycheiniog, the land of Brychan. The territory, centred around the fertile valley of the upper River Usk and flanked by mountains, retained its position as an independent realm well into the tenth century thanks to Brychan and his many descendants. According to legend, the leader – of Irish ancestry – had a vast family of twelve sons and twenty-four daughters, most of whom led religious lives. Some, like Tydfil, were martyred (Merthyr Tydfil, on the southern border of the National Park, means 'the burial place of Tydfil').

devices. English and Welsh manors even shared grazing rights on the common pasture that is still a major feature of the Beacons. The largest changes occurred in the more arable eastern lowlands, where the Normans introduced a feudal system of farming and tenants worked directly for the lord of the manor.

But politically, this was a deeply troubled period in which conflict was inevitable. After the Norman baron Bernard de Neufmarché, William the Conqueror's half-brother, defeated the ruler of the Welsh kingdom of Brycheiniog, he built a motte-and-bailey castle on a low hill at the confluence of the Usk and Honddu rivers at Brecon. This became the seat of power for his new lordship, a sphere of influence strengthened by other strongholds at Hay, Bronllys and Talgarth.

Many of the early Norman castles were later rebuilt in stone. Bronllys is a text-book example. The original eleventh-century motte, or mound, would have been encircled by a timber palisade and topped by a wooden tower. In the thirteenth century, a round stone keep was built on the motte, an addition that has largely survived over the centuries. Other castles – such as the tumbledown fragments at Crickhowell and Llandovery – have fared less well. The stone castle at Brecon has also suffered. The site has been unceremoniously cut in two by a road, with one half incorporated into the fabric of the Castle Hotel.

Abergavenny Castle was the scene of an infamous deed in 1175 that underlined where true power resided in times of uneasy peace. The infamous Norman lord William de Braose invited the local Welsh chieftains to the castle to hear a fictitious royal proclamation, only to murder them in cold blood.

Unlike Abergavenny – or, for that matter, any other castle in the National Park – Carreg Cennen had a foot firmly planted in both camps, serving in its time both English and Welsh masters. And, as I have already intimated, it is also quite unlike any of the other castles in terms of its presence and position.

In pure military or architectural terms it's no masterpiece, yet its exposed, stumpy ruins are charged with a sense of the past that is almost palpable. The location also casts a spell. The castle is perched on top of a sheer 300ft (90m) cliff, overlooking the emptiness of the Black Mountain near the hamlet of Trapp.

Carreg Cennen's convoluted history includes capture by Welsh and Anglo-Norman forces, surrender to Owain Glyndŵr during the last uprising against England in the fifteenth century, and notoriety as a hideaway for thieves and robbers. Take a torch when you visit, for the spectacle isn't just confined to the surface. A narrow passageway cut into the cliff leads to a cave below the foundations of the castle in which prehistoric skeletons have been discovered.

The end of serious hostility in these parts is neatly epitomised by the historic site which dominates the little village of Tretower. The two-in-one Tretower Court and Castle marks the end of the troubled medieval period and the start of more settled times when greater attention could be given to home comforts and less to the business of defence. The earlier part of Tretower is a robust round keep, plainly military in purpose, dating from the twelfth century. Next door stands Tretower Court, a handsome manor house with exquisite woodwork, courtyard and gardens, which captures a flavour of gracious living in late medieval Wales.

Enthusiasts of ecclesiastical architecture will find much to fascinate – and enchant – them in the Beacons. At Cwmyoy in the Black Mountains there's a tipsy church whose wonky tower and walls, the victims of serious subsidence, are still standing: but for how much longer? St Mary's Priory Church in

Handsome Tretower Court, built in the later Middle Ages. Its earlier accompaniment, a medieval fort, stands close by

Abergavenny contains a remarkable series of effigies and tombs – described as 'a national treasure' – spanning many centuries. The isolated St Meugan's Church, near Pencelli, has remains of a fifteenth-century rood screen. But best of all is Partrishow, hidden in the hills north east of Crickhowell (you'll need a good map to find it), whose rood screen of Irish oak – possibly the finest in Wales – is a showcase for the skills of the medieval woodcarver.

It's easy to confuse Llanthony Priory with Llanthony Abbey. The former deserves the most attention. This spot, tucked away in the peaceful Vale of Ewyas (a place 'more adapted to canonical discipline than all the monasteries of the British Isles,' according to medieval chronicler Gerald of Wales), was discovered by the Norman knight William de Lacy. His hermitage subsequently became an Augustinian priory, evocative remnants of which remain – especially the row of pointed Early English archways which frame an unchanging scene. Quite what the austere monks would have made of the small hotel-cum-inn now built into the ruins is anyone's guess. Llanthony Abbey stands a few miles to the north at the hamlet of Capel-y-ffin. The

Llanthony Priory, locked away in the remote Vale of Eywas, occupies a site of Christian worship dating back a thousand years

monastery here (now in private ownership) was founded in the nineteenth century by Father Ignatius, a charismatic religious figure.

Brecon has played a central role in the religious life of the area for centuries. Its grand Cathedral Church of St John the Evangelist (for the Diocese of Swansea and Brecon) dates from the times of Bernard de Neufmarché. The Norman lord built a church here next to his castle on the hill which overlooks the town. Improved and extended over the years, the church as it now stands dates mainly from the fourteenth century. The many notable features within its richly furnished interior include a magnificent east window and vaulting, Norman font and rare triple piscina. A Heritage Centre tracing the history of the site is housed in an adjacent tithe barn.

THE BIRTH OF INDUSTRY

It might seem a long stretch from the horse-drawn plough of the Middle Ages to the first sparks of industrial activity. In fact, it was not such a yawning gap, for our ingenious ancestors were busy laying the foundations of the Industrial Revolution as early as the sixteenth century. Not that it affected the Brecon Beacons to any great degree, for most of the hard work occurred elsewhere, albeit within a stone's throw from what is now the southern boundary of the National Park.

The conjunction of iron ore, limestone, woodland (for charcoal) and – as technology improved – coal itself on the southern rim of the Beacons led to a rash of activity and the genesis of industrial south Wales. The Old Red Sandstones underlying the Beacons acted as a geological firewall, an effective barrier against the heat generated by the coal- and iron-bearing rocks immediately to the south. This Great Divide – mentioned in the introduction – is thrown into stark relief at Henrhyd Falls, a National Trust site near Coelbren.

The falls plunge unbroken for 90ft (27m), exposing a seam of coal in the cliffs. Cast your eyes south from this picturesque spot and you'll gaze across to an alien moonscape of open-cast mine-workings which cover the blasted hillsides around the old coal-mining village of Coelbren.

Industrialisation did make its presence felt within what is now the National Park – but only just. The Clydach gorge between Gilwern and Brynmawr had all the natural assets to encourage iron-making, a situation exploited as early as the seventeenth century. Simple water-powered devices and plentiful timber for fuel were, in

Open-cast coal mining at Coelbren, a stark reminder of the proximity of industry along the southern boundary of the National Park

later centuries, replaced by steam power and coal as Clydach's forges produced increasing amounts of iron sourced from the local rocks. Tramways and inclines were constructed, quarries were hewn into the steep hillsides and increasingly sophisticated blast furnaces were built. Evidence of this hectic activity can still be seen today, yet the gorge doesn't just attract industrial archaeologists. Despite its industrial past, it retains a surprising degree of natural beauty, especially in its magnificent beechwoods now protected as a National Nature Reserve.

Above: Pen-ffordd-goch pond at the summit of the Blorenge, a mountain which still bears scars of south Wales's industrial past
Opposite: The narrow-gauge Brecon Mountain Railway follows part of the old Merthyr Tydfil to Brecon rail route through the Beacons
Below: In parts of the Clydach gorge it's difficult to believe that this was once a thriving iron-producing centre

Other industrial remnants can be seen scattered across the southern boundary of the Park in places like Brynaman, Pontneddfechan and on the Blorenge mountain above Abergavenny, but they soon give way to the open hill country to the north in which the sheep farmer, as in previous generations, continues to shape the landscape. The most prominent semi-industrial incursion into the Brecon Beacons was an entirely benign one, today the source of much pleasure. The Monmouthshire and Brecon Canal was built between 1799 and 1812 to connect Brecon with Newport. At one time it transported coal, lime and wool, but nowadays is busy with holiday craft which cruise sedately along a scenic 35-mile (56km) route between Brecon and Pontypool.

No place in Wales – not even the high and mighty Beacons – was safe from the railway mania of the nineteenth century. The rush to build routes during the Age of Steam saw Brecon linked from the south with Merthyr Tydfil, from the west with Neath and from the east with Hay-on-Wye. In the case of the Merthyr route, closed in 1962, the leftovers of the vanished line are entirely pleasing. The narrow-gauge Brecon Mountain Railway, operating from Pant at the northern end of Merthyr Tydfil, runs along the old standard-gauge line to a halt deep in the Beacons, within walking distance of the highest peaks in the Park.

4 Land use, culture and customs

Top: Traffic jam in a country lane
Above: Most parts of the Beacons
are accessible to walkers
Opposite: Hill-sheep farm below Pen
y fan and Corn Du

Look out across the Beacons and you see a landscape shaped not just by the nature of the underlying rock and the great ice sheets which scooped, scoured and polished the surface. Its appearance has also been hugely influenced by the endeavours of Man the farmer.

For the most part, this is no wilderness (though you may be forgiven for thinking so when plodding across the barren, hostile expanse of the Black Mountain). Sheep have grazed on these hills and mountains for centuries, providing sterling service as an army of four-legged lawnmowers in keeping a wilderness of tangled vegetation at bay. In the more fertile, sheltered valley floors, an orderly patchwork of farmers' fields imposes an unnatural regularity on the landscape. To quote from the National Park authority: 'No part of the Park landscape is "untouched by man".'

In purely economic terms, there's a debate nowadays – thrown into even sharper focus by the foot-and-mouth crisis of 2001 – about the relative value of agriculture and tourism in the National Park. Certainly, it's safe to say that income from tourism and the service industries has increased substantially in the last twenty years. But in terms of land use, there's no argument: around 90 per cent of the Park's total area is designated as farmland of one kind or another.

Add forestry to this percentage (a subject which is covered in more detail later) and there's a total of 98 per cent of land which is either dedicated to agriculture or afforestation. These activities bring full-time employment directly to about 1,500 people and support the livelihoods of many more.

Most of the farmland is taken up with stock rearing – specifically hill-sheep and beef-cattle farming. There are also small amounts of arable farming, mainly the growing of crops – hay, swede and barley – for animal feed.

A WORKING LANDSCAPE

The imprints left on the landscape illuminate farming practice in the Beacons. As altitude increases, the lowland field patterns gradually lose their grip, transmuting from rigid boundaries around and above the valley floors to ragged delineations higher up, which fade completely into rough, unenclosed mountainside above about 1,500ft (450m).

On hill and upland farms, sheep and cattle are reared for sale as breeding stock or for fattening on lowland farms. The upland sheep are hardy animals, roaming freely away from the farm for most of the year in the high, open countryside. The extent of open common land in the Park (38 per cent of the total area of 519sq miles/1,344sq km) is not that much less than the area taken

Above: A typical, traditional sheep farm (Harry Williams, courtesy of the National Trust)
Below: Cultivated land in the lower reaches of the Beacons gives way to open mountainside higher up

up by enclosed agricultural land (49 per cent) – a reminder yet again of the importance to farmers in the Beacons of the commons on which they enjoy grazing rights. The cattle are lowland animals, mainly confined to the enclosed farmland at lower altitudes where the crops grown for winter feed are also cultivated.

All things change, sometimes for the worse. The Beacons have thankfully been able to avoid the agri-business blitzkrieg which amalgamates smallholdings into giant farms, rips out hedgerows and introduces environmentally-insensitive mechanised methods of farming. Most of the farms in the Park are still owner-occupied – and, in any case, the nature of the terrain here makes the Beacons far less vulnerable to the agri-steamroller than places like East Anglia. Not that there aren't worrying trends in the Park – the decline in rough grazing, the replacement of herb-rich meadows with a pastureland of rye grass which provides better grazing, the destruction of hedgerows and dry-stone walls and so on.

The Park's Management Plan proposes action on a wide front to counter environmental degradation, with a range of objectives including the conservation and reinstatement of traditional field boundaries and other features of high landscape value, and an enhancement of the landscape through sustainable management.

Even before the foot-and-mouth crisis of 2001, British agriculture was in deep difficulty. In this context, the Park's Management Plan expresses a concern

that there may be a loss of small family farms, with detrimental consequences for the landscape and environment. The Plan also identifies measures – such as the promotion of agri-environment schemes and the encouragement of diversification – to address this threat.

Managing change is a difficult business. As the Plan says, 'The National Park is not a museum'. In this living, working environment there has to be a balance between conservation and commercial realities. After all, it was the destructive efforts – in today's terms, anyway – of our Neolithic ancestors in chopping down the forests which laid the foundations for the glorious open countryside which nowadays characterises the Beacons and is cherished by many environmentalists.

WOODLAND AND WATER

Forests still exist in the Beacons, but today they mainly consist of alien conifers. To my mind, there will always be something intrusive about a conifer plantation, with its sharply defined boundaries, regimented rows of tightly-packed trees and gloomy, dead interior. Despite the Forestry Commission's best efforts in more recent years to soften the blow through more sympathetic ways of planting and the retention of broadleaved trees, a block of conifers invariably delivers a sledgehammer blow to the landscape. This applies especially to the Beacons, where plantations bring the Park's soaring, open spaces to a rude halt.

Around 13 per cent of the National Park is covered by woodland, about 9 per cent of which is commercial conifer forest (Forestry Commission and other bodies). The forests, planted in the 1930s, 1950s and 1960s, are to be found along the southern dip slopes of the Beacons at medium elevations. There are five main plantations: Glasfynydd in the foothills of the Black Mountain; Coed y Rhaiadr around Ystradfellte; Coed Taf in the central Beacons; Talybont off the Usk valley; and Mynydd Du in the Black Mountains. Other significant plantings include 1,980 acres (801ha) in Fforest Fawr. Taken together, they represent by far the greatest impact on the landscape of the Beacons in the last 100 years.

HEDGEROWS AND DRY-STONE WALLS

Hedgerows are in a much better state of health in the Brecon Beacons than in many other parts of the country. This is due to local circumstances. Because the farming here is mainly stock-rearing, there has been far less removal of hedgerows than in lowland Britain, where fields and farms have become more easily amalgamated. Hedgerows are valuable not just for their contribution in enriching the landscape but also for the way they act as busy 'highways' for wildlife.

But their survival is under threat, even in the Beacons. The decline in numbers working on farms has led to a corresponding decrease in traditional maintenance work. Properly laid hedgerows are more difficult and time-consuming to look after than a simple wire-and-post fence. In its efforts to preserve hedgerows, the National Park Authority offers farmers a free advisory service, working with the Countryside Council for Wales to make them aware of the grants that are available. This free advisory service also covers dry-stone walls. The Park has also entered into a local partnership called the 'Walls of Llangynidr' to provide training and encourage restoration – an initiative intended as a pilot scheme that will be replicated in other parts of the Beacons.

The art of the dry-stone waller

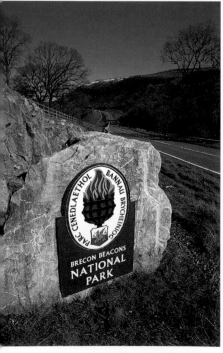

Broadleaved woodlands, alas, have not fared so well. There's now only a modest 12,500 acres (5,000ha) of oak, ash, birch, alder and others in the Park, substantially less than a century ago (in the Black Mountains, as much as 50 per cent of woodland was lost over a thirty-year period). One of the main desires expressed in the Park's Management Plan is that 'native broadleaved woodlands are extended'. The Plan aims to create 250 acres (100ha) of new native woodland per annum, as well as encouraging other broadleaved planting. It also sets out to counter the damaging effects of over-grazing and lack of regeneration and management by bringing 250 acres (100ha) of existing woodland a year into proper management.

Where there's wood, there's usually water – at least as far as the conifer plantations in the Beacons are concerned. Like the conifers, the water represents a significant – and relatively recent – change to the landscape: in this case in the form of reservoirs. There are eighteen in all, created before the National Park came into being and spread in a broad south-facing semi-circle from the Usk reservoir in the west to the Grwyne Fawr reservoir in the east. The main reservoirs are located in the central Beacons. The chain of three in the Taff Fawr valley, beside the A470 road, were created between 1892 and 1927 to supply Cardiff. Those in the Taff Fechan valley, dating from 1895 to 1927, supply the industrial valleys immediately to the south, while the Talybont Reservoir – at 2 miles (3km) long, the largest in the Park – supplies Newport.

Over the years, Talybont has become an important wildlife habitat, a role recognised by its status as a nature reserve. The passing of time has had a benign effect on many of these lakes, somehow softening their impact on the landscape. To my mind, they have brought fresh vistas and a welcome element of variety to their woodland and mountain settings. There's no denying the scenic appeal of reservoirs such as the Neuadd and Pontsticill in the Taff Fechan valley, set beneath the highest peaks in the Beacons, or the way in which high mountain ridges frame the generous spread of water at Talybont.

But eighteen reservoirs are sufficient, and the National Park would oppose any major new scheme unless there were very compelling reasons not to do so. The same stance applies to quarrying. The limestone outcrops along the southern rim of the Park bear witness to quarrying dating back to the time of the Industrial Revolution. Nowadays, only a handful of active quarries remain.

Above: The southern flanks of the Beacons are fringed with forests and reservoirs. The Talybont reservoir is one of the most scenic
Opposite above: Blocks of conifers have an unsettling influence on the open landscape of the Beacons
Opposite below: Entering the National Park north of Merthyr Tydfil

A MELTING POT OF CULTURAL TRADITIONS

The Brecon Beacons is very different to Snowdonia, its northern neighbour. Both are Welsh National Parks – but there the similarity ends. Their differences provide a clue to the difficulty that those who *really* know Wales have in coming up with a watertight definition of Welshness with which everyone, hand-on-heart, can agree. The Beacons, historically and geographically, have always had one eye – sometimes welcoming, at other times wary – on the border. Snowdonia, the mountain fastness to which the Welsh princes retreated

Wherever you travel in Wales, you'll see bi-lingual road signs

during the English invasions of the thirteenth century, has always been a stronghold of the Welsh culture and language.

The Beacons, lanced by major east–west through-routes and settled by Norman and Marcher lords almost from the time of the Conquest of 1066, have been more open to cross-border influences. The use of the Welsh language in the Park is a revealing barometer of such influence.

Take the two market towns of Abergavenny and Llandovery, at either end of the Park separated by a 40-mile (64km) trip along the A40. Abergavenny, at the eastern gateway, is a cosmopolitan country town where commuters and escapees from the Home Counties rub shoulders with farmers who talk in the broad vowels of the border. Llandovery, on the Park's western approaches, has an entirely different atmosphere. This is an out-and-out traditional farming town where you're more likely to hear Welsh being spoken.

It was near Llandovery, at the farmhouse of Pantycelyn, that one of the most influential members of the Welsh nonconformist movement lived. William Williams Pantycelyn (his place of abode was adopted as part of his name) was possibly Wales's greatest hymn-writer. 'Guide me, O Thou Great Jehovah' is his best-known composition, written like all his hymns originally in Welsh.

Nonconformism sprang from an innate radical tradition and disenchantment with the established Church, which was not perceived as meeting the needs of many Welsh people. Williams Pantycelyn was a leading figure in the great eighteenth-century Methodist Revival which swept across Wales, a status based not just on the strength of his composing abilities but also on his accomplishments as an indefatigable organiser and itinerant preacher.

In his old age he calculated that he had travelled nearly 150,000 miles and had spent almost as much time on horseback as at home. He died in 1791 and was buried at the church of Llanfair-ar-y-bryn in Llandovery, just off the A483 to Llanwrtyd Wells. His monument reads: 'He laboured in the service of the Gospel for nearly half a century and continued incessantly to promote it both by his Labours and Writings.'

The spark that ignited Williams Pantycelyn's religious fervour came from Hywel Harris, a charismatic preacher whose sermon at Talgarth converted Pantycelyn. Harris himself was fired by a vision at Talgarth's church in 1735, where he 'felt suddenly my heart melting like before a fire, with love to God my Saviour'. He was a fascinating figure. Not only did his preachings – delivered from a mobile pulpit to gatherings large and small – spearhead the great religious revival in Wales, but he was also an innovative farmer and social engineer.

At Trefeca near Talgarth he established a group or collective known as 'The Family' or 'Connexion' in which members pooled their resources for the common good, much in the way – in theory, at least – that the communes of the 1960s were supposed to operate. He introduced new farming methods and machines, and in 1755 founded the Brecknockshire Agricultural Society.

This remarkable, multi-talented man died in 1773 and was buried at St Gwendoline's Church, Talgarth, where a monument marks his achievements. The community Harris established at Trefeca, now a conference and retreat centre, contains a small museum dedicated to his memory.

The church at Llansantffraid near Talybont-on-Usk is the resting place of Henry Vaughan, who died in 1695. Vaughan, whose family hailed from nearby Tretower Court, was a metaphysical poet and doctor. He was known as 'The Silurist' after the Silures, the Celtic tribe that dominated south-east Wales

The tiny place of worship at Capel-y-ffin in the Vale of Ewyas

before the coming of the Romans. Vaughan's poetry, infused by a mystical view of nature, is thought to have influenced the work of William Wordsworth.

The Brecon Beacons have associations with an eclectic range of artists. The internationally-famous Victorian opera star Madame Adelina Patti was attracted to this area. An immensely wealthy artist who could command £1,000 per performance, she spared no expense in building Craig-y-nos Castle in the upper Tawe valley. Its appearance – a cross between a sham castle and Gothic château – perfectly encapsulates the flamboyant style of the times. Here, in the depths of Wales, she would entertain many illustrious friends and acquaintances, including royalty, and she even built into the house a bijou little theatre modelled on London's Drury Lane. The splendid 'pleasure grounds' that were created to accompany the mansion are now owned by the National Park authority and open to the public as the Craig-y-nos Country Park.

In the 1920s, sculptor and typeface designer Eric Gill sought solitude – and found it – at Capel-y-ffin in the remote Black Mountains, when he moved into a large, rambling house which was originally the monastery of the short-lived community founded by Father Ignatius, a nineteenth-century religious figure. Just across the valley is The Vision Farm, where writer Bruce Chatwin spent much time researching his best-selling book *On the Black Hill*, which captures the timeless nature of this forgotten corner of Britain.

Craig-y-Nos is a beautiful 40-acre (16ha) country park with lake, woodland and meadows set beneath limestone outcrops

THE LADY OF THE LAKE AND THE PHYSICIANS OF MYDDFAI

It's easy to let your imagination run riot on the shores of the inky-black waters of Llyn y Fan Fach in the misty, untrodden heights of the Black Mountain. The lake, cradled by the dark escarpment of the Carmarthenshire Fans, is the setting for a legend of a magical lady who rose from its waters. A local farmer fell in love with this Lady of the Lake. She consented to marry him with the proviso that, should he ever strike her three times, she would return to the waters. They lived happily and had five sons, but one day, by accident, the inevitable happened and she disappeared into Llyn y Fan Fach, leaving the broken-hearted husband and sons on the shore.

The sons and descendants of the ill-fated marriage became physicians who used the remedies taught by the Lady of the Lake. At this point, the legend becomes more intriguing, for fact begins to intertwine itself with fantasy. The healers did exist. In medieval times, the Physicians of Myddfai (a village near the lake) were famous throughout Wales for their healing powers and herbal remedies. Many of the cures seem strange, while others have stood the test of time. Some take the form of prophecy or advice. Ignore the following at your peril:

Suppers kill more than the Physicians of Myddfai can cure. If thou desirest to die, eat cabbage in August.

Pages 74–5: Myth-laden Llyn y Fan Fach in the Black Mountain

Very rarely do you come across places where conservation and recreation are obviously at each other's throats, but powerboating on Llangorse Lake is one. The Park considers it as something which disturbs the quiet appreciation of the lake, and a voluntary agreement exists to control this and other motorised watersports activities.

Another is caused by the celebrity status of south Wales's highest peak, Pen y fan, and the predictable attention it attracts. Walkers love the sense of openness and freedom which the Beacons impart. Perhaps in the case of the siren-like summit of Pen y fan, it's a case of a little too much love. What was forty years ago a single sheep track to the top has now become a downtrodden red furrow, the underlying soil vividly exposed and vulnerable to additional erosion caused by an annual rainfall of 90in (230cm). The peak's popularity is enhanced by its relative ease of access off the A470 at Storey Arms, a road that cuts through the heart of the central Beacons.

In all fairness, the National Park and National Trust have made sterling – and successful – efforts to stabilise the situation here through a sympathetic footpath repair programme. In this one particular battleground between conservation and recreation, an uneasy truce has, at least, been declared.

Sailing on Llangorse Lake

WALKING

Don't make the mistake of under-estimating the Brecon Beacons. These green hills and mountains look positively inviting in comparison to the brutish Scottish Highlands or the intimidating rockfaces of Snowdonia. In some ways, the Beacons have a hidden danger that other, more overtly severe, mountains don't possess: the capacity to induce complacency.

The fact that they are grassy and barely 3,000ft (900m) high, with summits that are flat-topped, gives them a benign air which is entirely unjustified. If you want the true picture ask the Special Air Services, or the Army. They use the Beacons for survival training. These mountains have claimed well-equipped and experienced victims, as well as walkers who perhaps didn't fully appreciate how challenging this high country can become.

Walkers approaching the peaks of the central Beacons, with the Neuadd reservoir in the background

The dangers are manifold. Mists descend with alarming rapidity. Flattish plateaux come to a sudden end in razor-sharp ridges and steep escarpments. A treeless, open landscape, so inviting on a warm summer's day, can be a nightmare in autumn and winter when you're vainly searching for shelter against an extreme wind-chill factor.

I'm as guilty as the rest when it comes to bagging the 'trophy peak' of Pen y fan. The view from the top, overlooking the glacier-scooped bowl of Cwm Llwch and beyond to Brecon and the hills of central Wales, is simply breath-taking. But I would recommend that you also look elsewhere in the Park, for there are many other places which are equally inspiring. As a quieter alternative to the western approach to Pen y fan from Storey Arms, you can reach the summit from the eastern side of the mountain, parking at the Neuadd reservoir and walking up the well-surfaced 'Gap route' before heading west along the ridge.

The Beacons may be a little beleaguered in one or two places, but essentially they still give you that rare and precious commodity: the space and opportunity to escape. You can walk for hours across huge tracts of mountainside, consistently above 2,000ft (600m), almost anywhere in the Park. Moorland, rolling hills and green valleys fringe the high country, offering a gentler type of walking. And as an antidote to the Beacons' big country with its big skies, there's the option of following shady trails through thick forests, or exploring the confines of wooded gorges in the 'Waterfall Country' of the southern limestone belt.

In walking terms, the character of the Beacons is defined by the fact that vast areas of open or common land – nearly 40 per cent of the total – make up the Park's area of 519sq miles (1,344sq km). There have been a few misconceptions about the freedom to roam on common land. Lawyers would no doubt insist on pointing out that common land is not in common ownership. Although local farmers have rights to graze their livestock on it, this land is privately owned.

In the Beacons we have been indeed fortunate over the years. While open country in other parts of Britain became disputed territory, the situation here has always been far less contentious. Though there was no legal right of access to common land (except, of course, on rights of way), actual – or *de facto* – unhindered access has usually applied here, with the proviso that farmers' rights are respected. As a further safeguard to public access it's good to report that a healthy percentage of the classic open scenery in the Beacons – including the central peaks and Mynydd Illtud common – is owned either by the National Trust or the National Park itself. In 1984, for example, the Park bought nearly 23,000 acres (9,300ha) of common land from the Eagle Star Insurance Company, a purchase that included Mynydd Illtud and the eastern portion of Fforest Fawr.

So historically there have been few obstacles to the enjoyment of the Beacons' exhilarating open spaces. And the future looks even rosier, for in December 2000 the Countryside and Rights of Way Bill became part of the law of Britain, granting the walkers their 'Holy Grail' of the right to roam freely in open country. It will not be legally enforced until around 2005; not that this represents too much of a problem in the Beacons, for it merely legitimises a situation that already applies in practice.

Walking is by far the most popular activity in the Park. Apart from the huge expanses of open countryside, there are over 1,000 miles (1,600km) of defined paths. Ask me for some of my favourite walks and I'll scratch my head, for it's a case of quantity and quality. For what it's worth, here are a few highlights, from east to west.

Begin your exploration of the Black Mountains at Llanthony Priory, following the track up to the ridge where you pick up the long-distance Offa's Dyke Path. When on top, it's an easy walk at a more or less consistent height of 2,000ft (600m) on a well-defined path to Hay Bluff, with spectacular views in all directions.

Opposite: The Garwnant Visitor Centre, in the forest beside the Llwyn-onn reservoir
Below: Inside the Brecon Beacons Mountain Visitor Centre

In the central Beacons, I'd recommend the classic ridge walk taking in Pen y fan, Corn Du and Cribyn, best approached – as already indicated – from the Gap road above the Neuadd reservoir. For a gentler alternative, follow one of the walks along Mynydd Illtud common from the National Park's Mountain Visitor Centre.

Fforest Fawr can be a little lonely and intimidating. But, thanks to the Romans, it is easily accessible when you follow sections of their ancient trackway known as Sarn Helen, which runs south westwards from Mynydd Illtud to Coelbren. The remote western Black Mountain is a true wilderness, regarded by many as having the toughest, most challenging terrain in the Park. You don't have to be a dedicated and determined walker to at least dip your toes into this environment – or, to be precise, into the icy

waters of Llyn y Fan Fach. One of my favourite walks here begins near the hamlet of Llanddeusant and follows the stony track up to myth-laden Llyn y Fan Fach, which sits beneath the escarpment of Bannau Sir Gaer at the gateway to the lost world of the Black Mountain.

Ystradfellte's 'Waterfall Country' is another favourite, with a magnificent riverside footpath beginning at Porth yr Ogof and running south past a series of spectacular falls. I don't want to give the impression that you need to be one of the stout-booted, map, compass and survival rations brigade to enjoy the great outdoors of this particular National Park. The Beacons are amenable to the most cartographically-challenged among us, with many gentle, waymarked walks suitable for all the family. Again, Mynydd Illtud is an eminently suitable place, as are the forests that clothe the southern slopes. The visitor centre at Garwnant above the Llwyn-onn reservoir is the starting point for a particularly well-developed series of forest trails; similar walks lead through the Taf Fechan Forest (where a boardwalk is suitable for wheelchairs) and from the head of the Talybont Forest to the lovely Blaen-y-glyn waterfall.

It's not difficult to find your way around. One of the best introductions to the area comes from the programme of guided walks run by the National Park, covering a wide variety of themes. Contact any information centre for details.

PONY TREKKING

The smooth, rounded profiles of the Beacons, devoid for the most part of the rocky gullies and crags you see in other mountain ranges, are ideal terrain for pony trekking. Gradual and relatively easy bridleways lead upwards into the commanding heights of the mountains, providing riders with an excellent choice of scenic trails.

Pony trekking is a pastime that can be enjoyed at all levels. Riding centres cater for everyone from beginners who want to sample a few hours in the saddle to experienced enthusiasts looking for a week's trekking inclusive of accommodation. No special kit is needed (hard hats are provided by the centre), though strong footwear is essential and warm windproof clothing,

TOMMY'S TALE

The Beacons, like any highland area, must be treated with respect. One poignant victim was little Tommy Jones. On 4 August 1900, five-year-old Tommy and his father, a miner from the Rhondda valley, set off to visit the child's grandparents who farmed in the Brecon Beacons. They arrived in Brecon by train, and walked south for 4 miles (6.4km) towards the remote farmhouse of Cwmllwch, located deep in the hills beneath the highest peaks of the Beacons. When almost at the farmhouse, and with night falling, Tommy became separated from his father. Soon, the Joneses and a group of soldiers training nearby began searching the mountain, but no sign was found of Tommy. Search parties continued to comb the area for the next few weeks without success.

The story captured the imagination of the public, and was reported in the Daily Mail, the newspaper offering a reward of £20 to anyone who could solve the mystery. Then a gardener's wife in Brecon is said to have dreamt of the spot where Tommy could be found. After a few fruitless searches, her husband found the body of poor Tommy on 2 September, high on the ridge above the lake of Llyn Cwm Llwch. The spot, now marked by a memorial, is 2,250ft (686m) above sea level, a difficult climb of a couple of miles from the safety of the farmhouse Tommy had almost reached. He had died of exhaustion and exposure.

waterproofs and gloves are advisable, even in summer when it can sometimes be unexpectedly cool on the hills. Ponies are Welsh cobs or cob-type, but some centres also have horses and cross-breds so that they can accommodate riders of any stature. Some centres also hire ponies for hacking or give riding instruction by the hour.

The Black Mountains are undoubtedly the favourite area within the Park for pony trekking, with a good spread of centres. There are also a few further west around Crickhowell and Llangorse, and one in the far west at Abercraf.

FISHING

This is a Park of rivers, lakes and reservoirs as well as mountains. Its main river, the Usk, is one of Wales's most famous fishing rivers, noted for its salmon and wild brown trout. Within Brecon there are several fishing platforms beside the river, with wheelchair access to two sites.

Two other celebrated fishing rivers, the Wye and the Tywi, border the Park. As well as salmon and brown trout, the Tywi's waters yield *sewin*, the local name for sea trout. Salmon, sea and brown trout can also be fished in the River Tawe, whose headwaters lie deep in the Black Mountain then flow southwards towards Abercraf. The River Honddu (in the Black Mountains in the far east of the Park, not the eponymous Honddu that flows into the Usk at Brecon) has brown trout and coarse fishing. The latter is also available on other rivers in the Park, notably the Usk and Wye.

In the limestone 'Waterfall Country' in the south west of the Beacons, the Rivers Hepste, Mellte, Neath and Pyrddin have brown trout with some

Opposite: Pony trekking is a popular pastime in the Beacons (Wales Tourist Board)
Below: Fishing for trout on the Cantref reservoir

salmon and sea trout, though the falls act as natural barriers to migratory fish in their upper reaches.

The many reservoirs along the southern, eastern and western flanks of the Beacons offer excellent fishing. On Talybont reservoir there's fly-fishing for trout. The Upper Neuadd reservoir, in a superb setting beneath Pen y fan, has a wild brown trout fishery (fly only). It's the first in a chain of reservoirs formed by the Taf Fechan river. Next comes Dol-y-gaer (otherwise known as Pentwyn), with its coarse and wild brown trout fishery, followed by Pontsticill, where you can fish for wild brown trout, pike, perch and roach.

The Taf Fawr river, which flows southwards towards Merthyr Tydfil from the heart of the central Beacons, has been dammed to form three reservoirs. The Beacons and Cantref reservoirs offer fly-fishing for rainbow and brown trout, while the southernmost reservoir, Llwyn-onn, has fishing for the same species, but extended to include fly-fishing, spinning and worming.

In the west of the Park, there's fly-fishing for wild brown trout on the Cray reservoir, while the remote Usk reservoir, hidden in the forest in a beautiful setting, has fishing for rainbow and brown trout. There are reserved areas here for disabled anglers.

Coarse fishermen are a familiar sight along the leafy banks of the Monmouthshire and Brecon Canal, which runs from Brecon, past Abergavenny to Pontypool. Perch, dace, carp and bream are among the fish that populate these ruddy waters.

For details on the appropriate fishing licences and permits, please contact local information centres.

CAVING

The caves in the Park's southern limestone belt are some of the longest and deepest in Britain. Cavers have explored over 20 miles (32km) of passageways at Ogof Agen Allwedd on the Llangattock escarpment above the Usk valley, for example. Ogof Daren Cilau, on the same escarpment, contains the largest cave passage in Britain, the Time Machine, around 100ft (30m) high and wide. The major system of Ogof Ffynnon Ddu near Abercraf in the upper Tawe valley contains Britain's deepest cave, 1,010 feet (308m) below the surface; it's also the second longest in Britain, extending for 28 miles (45km).

These and the many other caves in this area are potentially highly dangerous places and should only be entered by, or under the supervision of, experienced cavers. There are numerous caving groups active here; anyone who wishes to explore the caves further should get in touch with such a group. Major local libraries should be able to provide contact addresses.

There's one cave in the Beacons which makes spectacular viewing from the outside. Porth yr Ogof, near Ystradfellte, is the largest and most impressive cave entrance in Wales. Its giant mouth, around 65ft (20m) wide by 10ft (3m) high, opens out beneath a limestone cliff in a gloomy gorge carved by the River Mellte. A footpath leads down into the gorge from the car park above. But unless you're a properly equipped caver, don't be tempted inside.

This subterranean world isn't entirely out of bounds to the public. The Park's longest established tourist attraction is the National Showcaves Centre at the Dan yr Ogof Caves, Abercraf, which attracts around 65,000 visitors a year. The caves were first discovered in 1912, but their full extent did not become apparent until the late 1930s. Nowadays, the known passageways

extend for over 10 miles (16km), though cavers believe that the entire complex might well be double or treble this length.

Although the public have access to just a small part of this, there's nothing diminutive about its grandeur. Three separate caves are open: the original showcave, with its narrow passageways and strange formations, the aptly named 70ft-high (21m) Cathedral Cave and Ogof yr Esgryn (the Bone Cave) which interprets the archaeology and history of this area.

BOATING AND SAILING

Llangorse Lake, the largest natural lake in south Wales (around 1½ miles long by ½ mile wide), is a popular sailing and sailboarding venue, and dinghy racing takes place here on many Sundays. The enjoyment of the lake's peaceful beauty and wildlife is so important that the National Park is seeking some constraints over the type and extent of boating use, with the main objective of ending motorised watersports here.

The Llangorse Lake Advisory Group, on which the Park, boat owners, wildlife interests, fishermen and the lake's owners are represented, has drawn up an informal, self-regulating agreement. Powerboats (other than for water skiing), jet skis, jet bikes and water scooters are not allowed, but water skiing is permitted with limitations.

Dinghy and board sailors are also welcome at Pontsticill reservoir in the southern foothills of the Beacons. Like Llangorse, it has good slipway facilities.

The Rivers Usk and Wye attract increasing numbers of canoeists, especially in high water conditions: the Wye at Glasbury (where canoe hire is available) is a particularly popular stretch. Restrictions apply – please contact the Welsh Canoeing Association or any National Park information centre for details.

Canoeists are also a regular sight on the Monmouthshire and Brecon Canal, the inland waterway running for 35 miles (56km) between Brecon and Pontypool. The easiest places to access the canal are the Brecon terminus, the Pencelli slipway, Church Road in Gilwern and the Canal Junction, Pontypool. You can paddle your canoe along this waterway as rapidly – if that's the right word – as a motorised canal cruiser. These boats, varying in size from small open craft to traditional narrowboats with sleeping berths, chug along in their own placid, almost-pedestrian way. Boat and cruiser hire facilities are widely available, and places like Talybont-on-Usk and Gilwern, with their canalside pubs, are popular stopping-off places.

Left: The tranquil Monmouthshire and Brecon Canal
Right: Canoeists on the River Usk between Talybont and Llangynidr

The impression of effortless cruising along the Monmouthshire and Brecon is reinforced by the fact that it is a 'contour canal', so-called because it sticks wherever it can to a contour line above the Usk valley. Consequently there are no great changes in height – and only a handful of locks along the way to interrupt the journey.

Goytre Wharf is the location of the British Waterways' Canal Information and Sales Centre (tel 01873-881069). Short boat trips along the canal are available from the Brecon terminus and the Water Folk Canal Centre near Llanfrynach, which also has a canal museum.

MOUNTAIN BIKING

Mountain bikers love the Beacons. There are bridleways, RUPPs (roads used as public paths) and forest tracks to suit all levels of enthusiasm and fitness. There are so many classic rides in the Park that it is impossible to begin to describe them all here. The Hermitage green road, which climbs up the Grwyne Fechan valley in the hills east of Crickhowell, reaches a 2,027ft (618m) saddleback. This is followed by an adrenalin-inducing descent along the grass track that plunges down Mynydd Llysiau, its steepness indicated by the way the contours are squeezed together on the map.

The Roman road of Sarn Helen and the Gap route through the Beacons are well known, but there are many other rides of varying lengths and grades. Cyclists can also follow the section of the long-distance Taff Trail that runs from Cardiff to Brecon, signposted all the way. This route, a mixture of minor country roads and off-route tracks with good, firm surfaces, does not require any special riding skills and is suitable for families and occasional cyclists. Other undemanding off-road routes include some of the trails running from the visitor centre in the Garwnant Forest north of Merthyr Tydfil, and the section of the Monmouthshire and Brecon Canal towpath running from Brecon to Brynich Lock. There are bike hire facilities at Garwnant and Brecon.

OTHER ACTIVITIES

The Beacons are not renowned for their rock climbing. The best climbing is to be found in the old limestone quarries along the southern rim of the Park. When conditions are right, certain mountain ridges soon attract hang gliders and parascenders. The Blorenge mountain above Abergavenny and Hay Bluff are two particularly good spots. There is a gliding club near Pengenffordd between Talgarth and Tretower.

Left: Climbing at Craig y Ddinas, Pontneddfechan
Right: Cradoc Golf Club enjoys a wonderful setting, with views across to the central Beacons

6 Exploring the Park

ABERGAVENNY

This prosperous market town, flanked by the three peaks of the Sugar Loaf, Blorenge and Skirrid-fawr, is situated at the eastern gateway to the National Park. For once, the cliché 'old and new' rings true; Abergavenny remains faithful to its farming and rural past (the weekly livestock market is held each Tuesday, together with a big general market) while at the same time serving as a popular commuting town for those with jobs in urban south Wales. This cocktail of cosmopolitan with a twist of country gives Abergavenny a lively and appealing air. Away from the busy main shopping street, the River Usk flows quietly through grassy meadows.

On a bluff overlooking the river are the ruins of Abergavenny Castle, a medieval fortress which witnessed a black episode in Welsh history in 1175 when the infamous Norman lord, William de Braose, invited unsuspecting Welsh chieftains to a banquet, only to murder them while they were disarmed. In later centuries, parts of the castle were added to; an excellent local museum is housed in its nineteenth-century hunting lodge. The nearby Linda Vista Gardens also enjoy a pleasant setting and river views.

The most distinguished building in the town centre is the Victorian town hall, home of the local theatre and a covered marketplace, where craft and antique fairs are regularly held. Nearby St Mary's Priory has one of the finest collections of medieval effigies and monuments found in any church in Britain. There is a Tourist Information Centre and National Park information centre in the town.

Abergavenny is a prosperous shopping centre

BETHLEHEM

Tiny Bethlehem has a post office which is kept far busier franking collectors' first-day covers and special Christmas mail than serving the locals. The hamlet, between Llangadog and Llandeilo, takes its name from its chapel. Nearby is Carn Goch, a little-known – but surprisingly well-preserved – Iron Age hillfort, one of the largest in Wales.

BLAENAVON

This old industrial town, at the head of the eastern valleys, preserves its heritage well. In 1980, the local mine closed. But instead of being dismantled and sealed off, the colliery soon reopened to the public as the Big Pit Mining Museum. Visitors wear protective headgear and miners' lamps and are taken 300ft (90m) underground to 'pit bottom' for a guided tour. There's also much to see on the surface, including the engine house, miners' baths and workshops.

The town also pays homage to south Wales's metal-producing past at Blaenavon Ironworks (in the care of Cadw-Welsh Historic Monuments). Blast furnaces and workers' cottages have been preserved at this late eighteenth-century site, a milestone in the history of the Industrial Revolution. Blaenavon's exceptional iron- and coal-producing history was recognised in late 2000 when the town was declared a UNESCO World Heritage Site.

BRECON

Brecon, more or less equidistant from the eastern and western extremities of the National Park and overlooked by the peaks of the central Beacons, is a popular tourist centre. It's a handsome town of Georgian frontages and narrow alleyways, with a shopping centre largely untouched by the standard architectural package which has robbed so many places of their individuality. A sympathetic architectural touch is also much in evidence at the new, red-bricked Theatre Brycheiniog, which suits its canalside location eminently well.

Above: Remains of Brecon's medieval castle overlook the town
Opposite: The highest peaks in south Wales dominate the skyline above the handsome town of Brecon

A ruined castle, founded by the Norman lord Bernard Newmarch, stands on the hill above the confluence of the Rivers Usk and Honddu. On the same ridge is Brecon Cathedral, which began life as a Benedictine priory in 1100. The history of this significant religious site is recalled in an adjacent heritage centre.

Brecon is well blessed with two excellent museums. First is the Brecknock Museum, once the assize court, which traces the history of this area from prehistoric times. The South Wales Borderers' Museum is packed with military memorabilia, including items from the regiment's involvement in the Zulu War and the heroic defence of Rorke's Drift.

The town stands at one end of the Monmouthshire and Brecon Canal, which originally connected Brecon to the sea at Newport. There are boat trips run from the renovated canal basin, an attractive spot that is also the starting point of a towpath open to walkers and cyclists. There's another extremely pleasant walk at the opposite end of the town, running along a promenade beside the Usk to a boating station. A few miles west of the town in farmlands alongside the Usk are the ruins of Y Gaer, once an important Roman fort.

As well as serving as an administrative headquarters of the National Park, the town has an information centre for the National Park (part of the Tourist Information Centre). Market days are Tuesday and Friday.

BRONLLYS

Bronllys Castle is a single, cylindrical tower crowning a steep earthen mound. This simple but effective structure, put up in the mid-thirteenth century, replaced the original timber stronghold. The views from the top, overlooking the River Llynfi and the escarpment of the Black Mountains, are spectacular. The site is in the care of Cadw-Welsh Historic Monuments.

CAPEL-Y-FFIN

Isolated Capel-y-ffin is locked away in the Vale of Ewyas, a remote valley deep in the Black Mountains. Author Bruce Chatwin captured the spirit of this timeless, slightly spooky valley in his book *On the Black Hill*, written after a stay at a local farm. Two more enigmatic figures are associated with this area. Father Ignatius was a nineteenth-century religious man who built a short-lived monastery on the hillside above the hamlet; the monastery, now a private house, was later the home of artist Eric Gill. Capel-y-ffin itself is no more than a few dwellings grouped beside the Church of St Mary, a charming little doll's house which has been a place of worship dating from 1762. Beyond the hamlet, the narrow road through the valley climbs into the mountains to the summit of the Gospel Pass (yet more religious echoes), at 1,778ft (542m) the second highest road in Wales.

CLYDACH

Below: Underground spectacle at the National Showcaves Centre for Wales, Dan-yr-Ogof

The village stands at the entrance to the Clydach gorge, significant for its industrial heritage and natural beauty. The juxtaposition is a strange one: within the gorge there are remnants of eighteenth-century ironworks close to a National Nature Reserve created to protect magnificent beechwoods.

CLYRO

The Baskerville Arms makes the most of Clyro's reputed associations with Sir Arthur Conan Doyle and Sherlock Holmes. But we're on safer literary ground when we mention the fact that this pretty village, beside a lazy stretch of the River Wye, was once the home of the Reverend Francis Kilvert whose nineteenth-century *Diaries* captured the people and lyrical landscapes of the Welsh borders.

CRAIG-Y-NOS

The National Park's Craig-y-nos Country Park occupies the pleasure grounds of an ornate Victorian castle, home of the nineteenth-century opera diva Madame Adelina Patti (the castle is in separate ownership and not normally open to casual visitors). The 40-acre (16ha) park is a pleasing combination of river meadows, grassland, woodlands, lake and ornamental features, set beneath craggy limestone outcrops. There is an exhibition area in the park's visitor centre, which also serves as an information centre for the National Park.

Just across the valley is the National Showcaves Centre for Wales, where visitors can wander through three separate caves: the main Showcave with its narrow passageways, stalactites and stalagmites, the vast 42ft-high (13m) Cathedral Cave and the Bone Cave where archaeological displays trace the history of cave dwelling. This popular family attraction also has many above-ground features, including a dinosaur park, Iron Age village, museum, shire horse centre and adventure playground.

CRICKHOWELL

This small town in the Usk valley takes its name from Crug Hywell ('Howell's Fort'), the flat-topped summit – site of an Iron Age hillfort – which looms above the rooftops. There's a pleasing mix of architecture styles to be seen in this affluent little place: Georgian, traditional stone terraces, even mock medieval. For the real thing seek out the ruined Norman castle in the town park, or fourteenth-century St Edmund's Church. Crickhowell's best-known landmark is its many-arched sixteenth-century bridge across the Usk. A short distance out of town, beside the A40, are the remnants of a Neolithic (New Stone Age) burial chamber. There is a Tourist Information Centre in the town.

CWMYOY

The tipsy Church of St Martin at Cwmyoy continues to defy gravity. The victim of serious subsidence, it should by now have fallen down. Go there and wonder at its leaning tower, banana-shaped roof, crooked windows and buckled walls – before it is too late.

GILWERN

This large village, at the foot of the Clydach gorge, is a popular boating centre on the Monmouthshire and Brecon Canal.

The Bear at Crickhowell is a famous old coaching inn

GOVILON

Govilon is another convenient base for the Monmouthshire and Brecon Canal. The steep slopes of the Blorenge rise above the village, a mountain rich in industrial heritage and natural beauty.

HAY-ON-WYE

This pretty borderland town reinvented itself in the 1960s and 1970s. The turning point came with the opening of the first bookshop, and soon Hay changed from a sleepy backwater into the internationally famous 'town of books'. At the last count, there were around thirty bookshops here, selling expensive antiquarian tomes and pile-them-high second-hand books, discounted new novels and specialist books on everything from archaeology to zoology.

In the wake of this success story, antique and craft shops, bistros and cafés have also opened here, giving Hay an unexpectedly cosmopolitan atmosphere quite different to other country towns (it's always open, even on the darkest Sunday in deep midwinter). Hay's chic character is most apparent in late spring, when some of the world's top writers – and, it seems, the entire population of trendy north-west London – descend on the town for its prestigious Festival of Literature.

If visitors can tear themselves away from the bookshops they will discover a town of terraced stone cottages and steep streets, centred around an old covered market and overlooked by a part-ruined castle-cum-mansion. There is a Tourist Information Centre here.

Opposite: Hay-on-Wye has reinvented itself as the 'second-hand book capital of the world'
Below: The Merthyr Tydfil to Brecon A470 cuts through the heart of the Park

LIBANUS

Follow the signs from Libanus on the A470 south of Brecon for the National Park's Visitor Centre, which stands on Mynydd Illtud common and commands superb views of the central Beacons. It's full of information on what to see and where to walk, and is the best starting point for any visit to the Park.

LLANDDEUSANT

You only pass this way if you are seeking out the remote lakes of Llyn y Fan Fach and Llyn y Fan Fawr which lie beneath the northern escarpment of the Black Mountain. The hamlet's medieval church of two saints, St Simon and St Jude, stands on the site of a much earlier monastic community.

LLANDEILO

Llandeilo still makes its living as a country town serving the prosperous and productive Vale of Tywi. The lords of Dinefwr, ancient rulers of south Wales, presided over their kingdom from Dinefwr Castle. The castle, now in ruin, stands just west of the town next to the National Trust property of Dinefwr, a landscaped Capability Brown parkland created around Newton House, a seventeenth-century building with a Victorian Gothic façade.

Nearby Carreg Cennen Castle is undoubtedly the most spectacular medieval fortress in the National Park, if not Wales. Carreg Cennen's weatherbeaten defences cling to a precipitous rocky outcrop in the foothills of the Black Mountain. Its battlements, built

into a sheer cliff, command views far and wide. Carreg Cennen is an inspiring place to visit, not least for the memorable experience of walking through the narrow passageway carved into the cliff which leads to an underground chamber where prehistoric skeletons were discovered.

Both Dinefwr and Carreg Cennen castles are in the care of Cadw-Welsh Historic Monuments. There is a Tourist Information Centre in Llandeilo.

Above: Llandeilo stands on a rise above the Vale of Tywi
Below: Llandovery's attractive cobbled market square

LLANDOVERY

Nineteenth-century author George Borrow called Llandovery 'about the pleasantest little town in which I have halted' in his classic travel book *Wild Wales*. It's still an amiable place: cobbled market square, ruined castle, clock tower and inviting pubs and inns. The Llandovery Heritage Centre (part of the town's Tourist Information Centre) has displays on local history and wildlife, including the red kite. It also serves as a tourist and National Park information centre.

LLANGATTOCK

This village, on the Monmouthshire and Brecon Canal and just across the Usk from Crickhowell, takes its name from the Church of St Cattwg (*llan* meaning 'church'). Within this ancient church there are some exceptionally fine memorial tablets. The limestone escarpment above the village is noted for its cave systems and the Craig y Cilau Nature Reserve.

LLANGORSE

The village, ½ mile from the eponymous lake, is a pretty cluster of cottages which has developed around the Church of St Paulinus, a Norman church which occupies a much earlier Christian site dating back to the sixth century. Nearby Llangorse Lake, 1½ miles long, is the largest natural lake in south Wales. It lies in a flattish basin of land, set against the backcloth of the central Beacons. It's a popular spot: visitor and watersports facilities are concentrated along the northern shore, leaving the southern side of the lake peaceful and undeveloped. Llangorse's waters and reedy shores, an important wildlife habitat, are protected by a voluntary agreement between the National Park and the users of the lake.

The lake supposedly covers a legendary city. Lake dwellers did once live here: their small crannog, or artificial island, can still be seen.

LLANSANTFFRAED

Poet Henry Vaughan (1621–95), an influential figure in the Metaphysical movement, is buried in the roadside church at Llansantffraed. He lived at nearby Tretower Court (see separate entry).

LLANTHONY

Founded in the twelfth century as a spiritual retreat, Llanthony Priory was described as a place 'truly calculated for religion'. Over 800 years on, it's still difficult to disagree with this statement. The sense of peace surrounding the priory's serene ruins, set in the remote Vale of Ewyas, is almost palpable. An avenue of pointed Early English archways – the priory's finest feature – frame an unchanging scene of hill-sheep-farming country rising into the heights of the Black Mountains, Offa's Dyke and the Wales/England border. Incongruously, there's a tiny hotel-cum-pub built into the ruins, a hostelry much appreciated by thirsty walkers.

The priory, in the care of Cadw-Welsh Historic Monuments, is a good starting point for walking sections of the long-distance Offa's Dyke Path.

MERTHYR TYDFIL

The former iron and steel capital of the world stands at the southern approach to the Park. The town's influential role in the Industrial Revolution is recalled at the Ynysfach Iron Heritage Centre, housed in an early nineteenth-century engine house. Nearby, in a row of tiny dwellings once inhabited by ironworkers, there's Joseph Parry's Cottage, where Parry's life as a composer of many great Welsh hymns is recalled.

The ironmasters lived in considerably more comfort and style. Cyfarthfa Castle, set imperiously in its own grounds, was the home of the all-powerful Crawshay family. Their mock-baronial pile now serves as an excellent museum and art gallery. Pant, on the northern rim of Merthyr, is the terminus of the Brecon Mountain Railway, a scenic narrow-gauge line (one of the Great Little Trains of Wales) that runs into the foothills of the Beacons. Also north of the town (signposted off the A470) is the Garwnant Visitor Centre, starting point for walks and cycle paths along a network of forest trails. There is a Tourist Information Centre in the town.

Above: Detail from Partrishow's rood screen

Opposite: Storey Arms, highly accessible and located on the easiest approach to Pen y fan, has inevitably become a popular spot

Pages 100–1: Remote Partrishow Church, with its magnificent rood screen, is well worth seeking out

PARTRISHOW

You'll have difficulty finding Partrishow on the map. This scattered hamlet, deep in the hills north east of Crickhowell, is listed here because of its magical little church. Dating from the eleventh century, it boasts one of Wales's finest rood screens, intricately carved by craftsmen in Tudor times. Not quite so appealing is the figure of a skeleton painted on the wall, depicting death.

PONTNEDDFECHAN

This Vale of Neath village is a popular starting point for a number of walks which venture north along wooded riversides into the limestone Waterfall Country of the Beacons. In addition to falls and wooded gorges, there is an unusual walk along the Rivers Mellte and Sychryd to abandoned gunpowder works and silica mines. Also of special interest is the Craig y Ddinas rock, a geologically significant outcrop caused by a large fault. The village has a Tourist Information Centre.

PONTYPOOL

The old iron- and tinplate-making town of Pontypool stands at the far southern approach to the Park where the boundary dips onto the eastern valleys. The area's industrial part is the theme of the Valley Inheritance Museum, housed in Georgian stables in Pontypool Park. The Monmouthshire and Brecon Canal runs from Brecon to the Pontymoile Canal Basin, with its aqueduct and tollkeeper's cottage.

STOREY ARMS

On the crest of the busy A470 between Merthyr Tydfil and Brecon, Storey Arms has inevitably become a popular stopping-off spot, especially on summer weekends. First-time visitors may be disappointed by the lack of facilities – there is no pub here, nor anything else for that matter except a car park and outdoor pursuits centre. Storey Arms was named after landowner Story Maskelyne, not an inn. The most popular – and well-worn – path to Pen y fan starts from the roadside. It's a fairly uninspiring slog up the mountainside to the flat-topped summit. If you know your way around the mountains there's a far more rewarding approach to the summit from the Neuadd reservoir north of Pontsticill.

TALGARTH

Talgarth has never quite managed to keep up with its more go-ahead neighbours. Despite an enviable location at the foot of the Black Mountains, it does not share the popularity with visitors that Brecon or Hay-on-Wye enjoys. St Gwendoline's Church is a significant religious site. It is associated with Hywel Harris, a remarkable man who led the eighteenth-century Methodist Revival in Wales. Harris established a community in nearby Trefeca, based not only on religious principles but also on ideas about communal living and innovative farming practices, which were very progressive for their time. There is a Tourist Information Centre here.

TALYBONT-ON-USK

Canal cruisers, mountain bikers and fans of real ale all share an affection for this village. The Monmouthshire and Brecon Canal flows through Talybont; cycle trails run from the village up into the forests and on to the high Beacons; and there are lots of excellent pubs. The only downside is in the misleading name: Talybont isn't actually on the Usk – the river is about half a mile away. Talybont reservoir, in the hills to the west of the village, has become an important habitat for birdlife, especially winter populations of wildfowl. The National Park's Danywenallt Study Centre is located close to the reservoir. Based at a converted farmstead which enjoys stunning views of the surrounding hills and nearby reservoir, the centre offers a wide range of courses to groups.

TRETOWER

Tretower's historic claim to fame resides in its court and castle, an unusual two-in-one site. The castle is the oldest, a stark, simple round tower put up in the troubled twelfth century when life was full of threat. In the later, more settled, fourteenth and fifteenth centuries greater attention could be given to home comforts, hence the magnificent Tretower Court, a fortified manor house, rare in Wales, which displays superb evidence of late-medieval craftsmanship in wood and stone.

Tretower Court was the home of Henry Vaughan, the seventeenth-century poet who is buried at nearby Llansantffraed Church. The site is in the care of Cadw-Welsh Historic Monuments.

YSTRADFELLTE

This hamlet – no more than a church, pub and handful of houses – is better known than its size suggests. Its name is synonymous with the National Park's Waterfall Country. All the classic limestone features are to be found within a few miles of Ystradfellte – the stumpy outcrops, the deep gorges, the potholes, caves and falls. Just south of the river is Porth yr Ogof, a gaping cavern which swallows up the River Mellte. From the car park at the cave there is a footpath downstream which leads to a spectacular series of waterfalls.

Opposite: There's an attractive walk through the woods to the Blaen-y-glyn waterfall at the head of the Talybont Forest

Pages 106–7: Two historic sites for the price of one: Tretower's medieval keep stands close to a fine Court, built in later, more peaceful times

Information

USEFUL ADDRESSES

Brecon Beacons National Park
  Authority
7 Glamorgan Street
Brecon LD3 7DP
Tel: 01874 624437
email:
enquiries@breconbeacons.org
www.breconbeacons.org

National Park Study Centre
Danywenallt
near Talybont-on-Usk
Tel: 01874 676677
email:
danywenallt@breconbeacons.org

NATIONAL PARK VISITOR CENTRES

Brecon Beacons National Park
  Mountain Centre
near Libanus
Tel: 01874 623366

Craig-y-nos Country Park
near Abercraf
Tel: 01639 730395
email: cyncp@breconbeacons.org

Abergavenny Information Centre
Monmouth Road
Abergavenny NP7 5ER
Tel: 01873 853254

Brecon Information Centre
Cattle Market Car Park
Brecon LD3 8ER
Tel: 01874 623156

Llandovery Information Centre
King's Road
Llandovery SA20 0AW
Tel: 01550 720693

National Park Village Information Agencies
are located at:
Abercraf (The Village Shop);
Brynaman (Siop-y-Dyffryn);
Govilon (Post Office);
Llanddeusant (Cross Inn and
Black Mountain Camping Site);
Llanfihangel Crucorney (Post
Office); Llangynidr (Llangynidr
Service Station and Post Office);
between Pontneddfechan and
Ystradfellte (Rhos Filling Station
and Shop); Sennybridge (Spar
Shop); and Talybont-on-Usk
(Post Office and Stores).

TOURIST INFORMATION CENTRES

There are TICs at:
Abergavenny
(Tel: 01873 857588)
Brecon (Tel: 01874 622485)
Crickhowell (Tel: 01873 812105)
Hay-on-Wye
(Tel: 01497 820144)
Llandeilo (Tel 01558 824226)
Llandovery (Tel: 01550 720693)
Merthyr Tydfil
(Tel: 01685 379884)
Pontneddfechan
(Tel: 01639 721795)
Talgarth
(Tel: 01874 712226)

OTHER BODIES

Cadw-Welsh Historic
  Monuments
Crown Building
Cathays Park
Cardiff CF10 3NQ
Tel: 029 2050 0200
www.cadw.wales.gov.uk

Countryside Council for Wales
Plas Penrhos
Fordd Penrhos
Bangor LL57 2LQ
Tel: 01248 385500
www.ccw.gov.uk

Forest Enterprise (Forestry
  Commission)
Victoria House
Victoria Terrace
Aberystwyth SY23 2DQ
Tel: 01970 612367
www.forestry.gov.uk

National Trust Wales
Trinity Square
Llandudno LL30 2DE
Tel: 01492 860123
website:
www.nationaltrust.org.uk

Offa's Dyke Association
West Street
Knighton LD7 1EN
Tel: 01597 528753
website:
www.offa.demon.co.uk/offa.htm

National Caving Association
c/o Monomark House
27 Old Gloucester Street
London WC1N 3XX

ATTRACTIONS

Abergavenny Castle and Museum
Castle Street
Abergavenny
Tel: 01873 854282

Big Pit Mining Museum
Blaenavon
Tel: 01495 790311

Blaenavon Ironworks (Cadw-
Welsh Historic Monuments)
Tel: 01495 792615

Brecknock Museum and Art
Gallery
Captain's Walk
Brecon
Tel: 01874 624121

Brecon Cathedral and Heritage
Centre
Brecon
Tel: 01874 625222

Brecon Mountain Railway
Operates from terminus at Pant
just north of Merthyr Tydfil
Tel: 01685 722988

Carreg Cennen Castle (Cadw-
Welsh Historic Monuments)
Trapp
near Llandeilo
Tel: 01558 822291

Cyfarthfa Castle Museum and
Art Gallery
Merthyr Tydfil
Tel: 01685 723112

Dinefwr (National Trust)
Llandeilo
Tel: 01558 823902

Garwnant Visitor Centre
In Coed Taf Forest off A470 a
few miles north of Merthyr
Tydfil
Tel: 01685 723060

Hywel Harris Museum
Trefeca
near Talgarth
Tel: 01874 711423

Llangorse Rope Centre (indoor
climbing)
Llangorse
Tel: 01874 658272/658584

Llanthony Priory (Cadw-Welsh
Historic Monuments)
Llanthony
(no telephone – free access)

The National Showcaves Centre
for Wales
Dan-yr-Ogof
Abercraf
Tel: 01639 730801
www.showcaves.co.uk

South Wales Borderers' Museum
The Barracks
Brecon
Tel: 01874 613310

Tretower Court and Castle
(Cadw-Welsh Historic
Monuments)
Tretower
Tel: 01874 730279

Valley Inheritance Centre
Pontypool
Tel: 01495 752036

Water Folk Canal Centre
Old Storehouse
Llanfrynach
Tel: 01874 665382

MAPS

The use of the appropriate
Ordnance Survey maps is highly
recommended for any detailed
exploration of the National Park.
The ones which cover the area of
the National Park are:

Outdoor Leisure Maps
(1:25,000): Nos 11, 12 and 13,
the Central, Western and Eastern
Brecon Beacons respectively.
Landranger (1:50,000): No 160
Brecon Beacons, No 161
Abergavenny and the Black
Mountains.

FURTHER READING

Condry, William. *Wales* (Gomer Press/The National Trust, 1991)

Howell, Peter, and Beazley, Elisabeth. *The Companion Guide to South Wales* (Collins, 1977)

Houlder, Christopher. *Wales: An Archaeological Guide* (Faber and Faber, 1974)

Mason, Edmund J. *Portrait of the Brecon Beacons* (Robert Hale, 1975)

Thomas, Roger. *Great Walks, Brecon Beacons and Pembrokeshire Coast* (Ward Lock, 1989)

Thomas, Roger. *A Complete Guide to South Wales* (Jarrold Publishing/Wales Tourist Board, 1997)

Various authors. *Ordnance Survey Leisure Guide, Brecon Beacons and Mid Wales* (Automobile Association/Ordnance Survey, 1989)

In addition, the Brecon Beacons National Park Authority publishes a comprehensive range of reasonably priced titles, covering everything from archaeology to walking.

Index

Page numbers in *italics* indicate illustrations